FUR
TRAPPING

WINCHESTER PRESS

An Imprint of NEW CENTURY PUBLISHERS, INC.

FUR
TRAPPING

BILL MUSGROVE
GERRY BLAIR

Printing code
11 12 13 14 15 16 17
Library of Congress Catalog Card Number: 82-63153

ISBN 0-8329-0334-5
Printed in the United States

Contents

Foreword

This book deals with the trapping, killing, and skinning of wild animals and the selling of their pelts. It is intended as an honest book, one that talks about fur trapping—not taking, or harvesting, or catching, but trapping. It has become fashionable in recent years to avoid such strong words as trapping, killing, bleeding, and shooting, but this approach is not ours. Trapping is an honorable profession, and we will refer to trappers as trappers. And when it comes time to kill a trapped animal, we will be honest in our terminology there, too.

To those who disagree with this outlook we offer no apologies. We are convinced that fur trapping is both necessary and humane. Trapping is necessary from a game-management aspect to maintain a balance between wild animals and their habitat. When left uncontrolled, the numbers will multiply and overkill prey species. Predatory animals will then turn to domestic stock and poultry. Small and large game animals will be eaten. Many furbearers, when their numbers are too high, die of disease and starvation. Many, such as the skunk, the coyote, the fox, and the bobcat may contract rabies and become a threat to humans and their pets.

Trapping an animal in a leghold trap, we feel, is no less humane than the slitting of a chicken's throat, the bludgeoning to death of a steer, hog, or sheep, or the slow starvation of a predator who has over reproduced to the point that his habitat will no longer support his numbers.

We see fur trapping, as a hobby or as a profession, to be more attractive than the predator-control trapping done by agencies of state and federal governments. Such trapping, done at taxpayer expense, is a total waste of a natural resource. We see citizen trapping as more humane than massive poison campaigns which sometimes destroy entire food chains. We see the leghold trap as more desirable than so called killer traps that destroy target and nontarget catches indiscriminately.

To those who are attempting fur trapping for the first time, we bid you welcome. You are embarking upon an honorable pursuit of game that is closely tied to the economic development of this country. You will be walking the tracks and trails of frontier giants. James Bridger, Kit Carson, and a hundred others were trappers. The knowledge they gained of the Western frontier permitted emigrant travel, the construction of railroads, and a peaceful coexistence with many Indian tribes.

The back country, the quarry, and the method of trapping has changed but little the past hundred or so years. You will trap as they trapped, outwitting the quarry on his home ground. It is our hope that this book will make your trapping experience rewarding, healthful, and enjoyable. Good Luck!

Bill Musgrove
Gerry Blair
November, 1978

1
Fur Trapping Today

Fur trappers in the United States shared in more than $400 million during 1976. According to the U.S. Department of Commerce, the same agency that supplied the estimate on the total take, almost 2 million full-time and part-time trappers annually set their traps for predators such as coyote, bobcat, red and gray fox, and members of the weasel family. They also trap non-predators such as muskrat and beaver, and some half-dozen other animals whose fur is marketable.

Many of the trappers who take to the field each year are nonprofessional trappers who have no strong drive to make a large profit from their trapline. For the hobby trapper, either because he lacks time or because he lacks skill, it is enough just to get afield for a few hours each day. The occasional skunk or muskrat he collects from his line is enough to satisfy him and pay for the few supplies needed to operate the line. A farmer or rancher may also be an occasional trapper—trapping mainly to reduce or eliminate species he may consider destructive to crops or livestock. He may be a good trapper in the sense that he knows the quarry and knows the land, but he traps more for self-preservation than for profit.

In the strictest sense, a homeowner in the suburbs who traps a pesky gopher from his tulip bed is a hobby trapper. So is the little old lady who lives in a city apartment and uses a trap to rid her kitchen of rats or mice.

Some trappers, on the other hand, are professionals—they run their lines for profit. They are businessmen, just as the corner grocer is a businessman. They know how to catch furbearers, they know how to skin each species so as to bring the best price, they know how to clean, stretch, and repair fur, and they know when and where to market their product. This is not to say that the professional trapper does not enjoy his trade. On the contrary, he usually derives immense enjoyment from his outdoor experiences. He traps for all of the same reasons that motivate a hobby trapper. The difference is, the professional, or money trapper, also makes a good healthy profit from his trapline. For the most part, hobby trappers will not take the time needed to be a topnotch trapper. They will not study the target animal until they are completely familiar with its habits and the peculiarities of its nature that make it vulnerable. They will not take the time to study the trapping territory until they are well acquainted with every scratching area of the cat, the community scent posts of the coyote, the mud slides of the beaver and otter, and the winter dens of the skunk. The ground, the water, and the trees hold a wealth of information for those who are willing to understand, and the professional trapper interprets these signs into an increased fur catch and a bigger payday at season's end.

Professional trappers are money trappers. They are willing to invest money in good traps—getting the right-size trap for the target animal, not trying to make do with a trap that may be too large or too small. They buy or make the correct type and size of stretcher for each species, and usually have three or four sizes of stretchers for a single species. By stretching each individual pelt to its maximum size, the money trapper gets the best price for each individual pelt.

In the early days of trapping a long-line trapper was one who ran a line so long that it could not be covered in a single day. Usually, the line took several days to run and the trapper would have waystations along the line to make his overnights. These were generally in the form of a crude line cabin, a lean-to, or if he was really roughing it, a sleeping bag laid on a carpet of evergreen boughs under the limbs of a friendly tree.

There are few long-liners left. Those who do survive do not walk their lines as the early trappers did. Instead, they use a vehicle, usually a four-wheel-drive. It would probably be correct to modify the definition of long-liner to include any trapper who devotes his full attention to the business of trapping. With a vehicle, and the right type of country, the modern long-liner can cover more ground in a day than his early counterpart did in a week. Most money trappers are long-liners under this definition.

The trapper should trap the fur most in demand. If bobcats bring a high of $400, as they did in 1976, he should concentrate on them. *(Photo: Gerry Blair)*

Their traplines may run from 50 to 200 miles, and most check their traps on the daily basis required by law in some states—and required for humane reasons everywhere.

The type of trapline should depend upon the availability of the game species in the area to be trapped. The current market for fur species should also be considered. If bobcats, for example, bring a high of $400, as they did during the spring of 1977, it would be bad business to spend much time setting traps for a low-demand species such as beaver. A well-set cat trap will also take other valuable furbearers, so the trapper may get a bonus in a catch that is nontarget in the strictest sense but still welcome. Gray fox, skunk, ringtail cat, and badger will come readily to a baited cat set.

Most country which offers a bobcat population also houses important numbers of coyote. As a general rule a coyote will not come to a cat set. There is always the exception to the rule, of course; an occasional dumb coyote will find itself with its foot caught in a No. 2 set for cat. Unless it is small in addition to being dumb it will not stay caught for long. The No. 2 is not a good trap for coyote; it is on the small side and most will pull out on the first jump. A coyote set, on the other hand, will also take bobcat. (Not a lot, but the ones caught seem to be the larger cats in the territory, and the careful trapper will realize a bonus of a dozen or so cats from his coyote sets each season.) To catch a coyote the trapper must have the coyote in mind when he sets his trap. Both types of set, one for coyote and one for bobcat, should be placed on the trapline.

So far we have been discussing trapping as a private hobby, business, and means of predator control, and that, of course, is the topic of this book. However, we should touch on *public* trapping—that is, trapping done by government professionals.

Government trappers are not after fur. They are employees of the county, state, or federal government who attempt to control livestock predation by reducing predator numbers. Many state game departments employ trappers to work problem areas as a game-management tool. Federal government trappers work for the U.S. Fish and Wildlife Service, a branch of the Interior Department. These federal trappers usually respond to rancher complaints of predation, and their target is usually one of the large predators—the coyote, the bobcat, the mountain lion, and more rarely, the black bear.

The government trapper, unfortunately, does most of his trapping during the hot months of the year when the fur is not prime. Too, regulations require that the fur not be sold. Many residents of the rural areas of the West have seen huge mounds of trapped coyote, fox, and bobcat piled high by the government trappers. These trappers use the steel leghold trap, the cyanide gun, and, on occasion, poison bait. Both the cyanide gun and the poison allow the animal to leave the scene of the trap before it dies. In the case of the cyanide gun, death will probably occur within 30 seconds. When a coyote or other predator pulls on the bait, a detonator cap fires a spray of deadly cyanide gas into the face of the animal. The fur is usually ruined soon after death. The strong stomach acids in a coyote will turn the stomach fur green in a matter of hours.

The catch of the government trappers, for the most part, will be the young of the current year. The youth of these animals makes them vulnerable to most types of traps. They have not lived long enough to become trap-wise. The animals left by the government trapper are the older and smarter animals. These will be the target of the money trapper who sets his line later in the year, and in many instances, they have received an education in traps from the government trappers.

A target of both government and private trappers. The coyote pelt peaked in price during the mid-'70s. A prime Colorado silver brought up to $70. *(Photo: Duane Rubink, U.S. Fish & Wildlife Service)*

Like any deliberate control method, government trapping has its critics, from those who think man should let nature completely alone to those who simply want every animal that remotely threatens their business activities wiped out. Neither extreme is worth discussing, but it might be worthwhile to explain why the government does have trapping programs.

Predatory animals, and the coyote in particular, play an important role in the determination of game-animal numbers. Careful government studies have proven that in some areas, herds of deer and antelope are far smaller than the carrying capacity of their range should permit, and that the cause is an excessive toll taken by predators. Reducing the predator population will permit the herds to increase. Predatory animals also make important inroads into the young of birds and small-game species. Quail, pheasant, grouse, and other ground nesters are easy prey for a hungry predator. So are cottontail rabbits, both adult and young; the young of the jackrabbit; and any other bird or animal that spends a good part of its time on the ground. Even waterfowl such as ducks and geese are not safe from a hungry predator. They are extremely vulnerable when they come to land to feed, nest, or rest. The adult bird may be attacked and taken, the nest may be robbed of its eggs, and after hatching, the young are easy game for any predator worth his fur. The coyote, fox, and bobcat are meat eaters, for the most part, and are highly efficient predators.

Predatory animals, again particularly the coyote, are also harmful to many domestic animals. Many sheep ranchers of the Western states have abandoned the business because coyote predation has caused it to be no longer profitable. Many times the coyote will attack a band of sheep and continue wanton killing until no sheep are left available to attack. The coyote is also a threat to the survival of beef animals. One Colorado rancher documented the loss of twenty-two newborn calves in a single season. The rancher was a small operator, with only one hundred head of cattle on his ranch, and the loss to predators spelled the loss of his profit for that year's work.

Residents of the suburbs of Tucson, Arizona, a city of almost 500,000, were recently plagued with a series of attacks on their household pets. When the killings reached epidemic proportions the homeowners called in wildlife experts from the Arizona Game and Fish Department. They at first suspected a large cat, perhaps a mountain lion or a jaguar. It was decided, however, that the attacking animal was a coyote, or perhaps more than one, who saw the dog as a tasty meal. Tucson also has had recent problems with rabid attacks on human residents. Eight such attacks were documented during the summer of 1977. The problem became so serious that county officials declared a rabies epidemic was present and placed an animal quarantine upon the county.

Thus the evidence is strong that predators do exactly as their name implies: They predate. They have their place in nature's scheme, and of course they are a source of income to the private trapper; they shouldn't be wiped out. But unusual numbers of coyotes can soon bankrupt a sheep or cattle rancher. Too many bobcat or fox can put the poultry growers out of business. Too many of either can seriously impair the population of game animals and drastically lower the hunter success ratio.

2
Steel Traps and Other Takers

Sewell Newhouse was a gunsmith by trade, and he was a good one. It was a profitable time to be a gunsmith. It was 1823 and such adventurous men as Kit Carson, Jim Bridger, and Bill Williams would soon head into the mountains to trap beaver. They needed good guns to take along to shoot grizzlies and to defend their traps and their lives from Indians. The Newhouse rifle soon gained fame as a companion that was good enough to take along.

It was natural, then, that some of the men who came to Newhouse for a rifle would talk to him about traps. There was trapping aplenty close to the Newhouse home at Oneida, N.Y., more trapping on the nearby Oneida Indian Reservation, and more yet across the line into Canada. Soon Sewell Newhouse perfected a trap design that brought him more business than his guns.

Newhouse's steel leghold was of a very simple design, yet it was reliable. One or two pieces of spring steel were bent to a U shape to provide the tension. Two steel jaws provided the holding ability, and a round piece of metal served as the triggering device. The design was so well planned that no significant change in this trap, usually called the longspring trap, has occurred in the more than 150 years since Sewell Newhouse made his traps.

Newhouse was particular about his traps. He knew that his reputation as a trap maker went with each trap he made. The temper of the traps had to be just right. If the steel became too hard the metal would be brittle and the trap jaws would break the first time that the trap was sprung empty. If the trap steel was too soft the spring, which was the heart of the trap, would soon go bad and the trap would not be worth setting. The jaws had to spring crisply

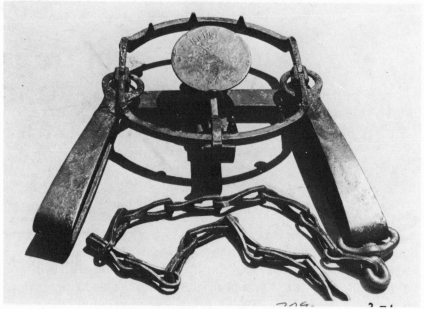

A longspring trap, double-spring, of traditional design. Traps with teethed jaws are no longer legal in most states. *(Photo: Gerry Blair)*

so that no animal had time to pull out as it felt the pan give. Not too crisp, however, as the legbone of the animal would break and allow a pullout. The pan dog was made narrow and thick—narrow so there would be little surface to grab the animal's foot and possibly throw it from the jaws, thick for strength.

The first Newhouse traps were these longspring traps, either single- or double-spring. As the demand for the traps grew, Newhouse was unable to meet the demand making the traps by hand. Soon a factory was built and the Newhouse traps were offered in sizes made to take anything from muskrat to grizzly bear.

As the years went by, other variations of the steel trap appeared. The underspring trap, or jump trap, was one. This design has a single spring that comes back under the jaws of the trap. When the trap is sprung, the placement of the spring causes the trap to rise, or jump, in the air and catch the target high on the leg.

Some traps were made to be specific for certain animals. The double-jaw and the webbed-jaw traps were made with the water animals in mind for the most part. Muskrat, beaver, and otter would often twist out of a trap if the set was not a drown set. The losses increased if the trap broke the legbone. The animals would twist the remaining flesh and gristle and would leave the trapper with nothing more than a foot for his efforts, poor wages to support a family. The double-jaw trap was made to prevent twist offs. The trap had two sets of jaws, one on top of the other. A trapped animal might chew under the lower jaw but could not reach the upper or main holding jaw. The webbed jaw served the same purpose. It had only a single set of jaws but the jaws were thick and flanged.

The jump traps, and the later coilspring traps, had a number of features that made them more attractive to the early trappers. They were smaller and lighter than the longspring traps, and more of them could be packed on the line. Most trappers then walked their lines, and the more traps they could carry, the bigger the catch and the payday. The traps also set flatter and were easier to conceal. An underspring or a coilspring trap could be set in places that would not accept a longspring trap.

Some of the early traps had features that were intended to increase the holding power of the trap, such as sawtooth jaws and spike jaws. Most states now outlaw this type of trap. Many trappers feel that these jaw modifications did nothing to increase the catch anyway. Modern trappers, for humane as well as legal reasons, would do well to avoid such traps.

There was even an early type of killer trap. It was called the tree trap and was nailed to a tree below a bait. When the animal disturbed the trigger, a large piece of metal, somewhat like the jaw of the common mousetrap, would be released and would pin the animal to the tree with killing force. It could be used, of course, only on animals that had the ability to climb the tree.

Other traps were even more narrow in their application. One trap was made to take an otter at an otter slide. The trap was made to grab the otter as it slid by, not by the foot as was usual, but by the loose skin of the body.

Soon the demand for steel traps induced other manufacturers to enter the trap market. Some were handmade, like the Newhouse traps, and others were mass-produced. The machine-produced traps were inferior, but they were much cheaper. When they hit the market, almost anyone could afford an outfit of traps. The mass-produced traps were not as strong and they would not last as long, but the price was right. Too, trap thieves were out and about

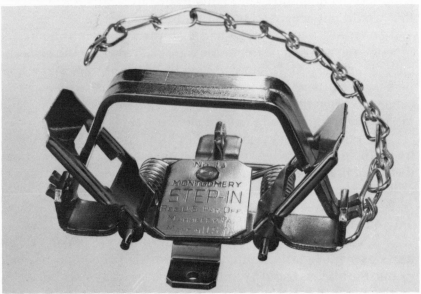

Some trappers prefer the coilspring trap as it is smaller and easier to conceal. *(Photos: Montgomery Traps)*

even then. Better to lose a mass-produced trap than to lose an expensive Newhouse.

There are just a few trap manufacturers in modern times. All offer a variety of trap sizes and trap designs. The longspring trap,

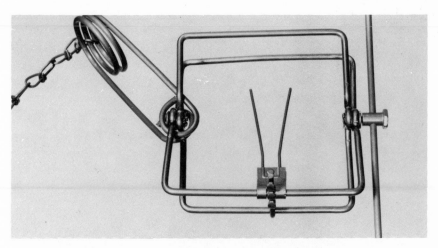

A killer trap of the Conibear type. The square jaws close on the animal's chest and kill by suffocation. *(Photo: Montgomery Traps)*

with both single and double spring, is still available. It is still a very popular trap. The underspring trap (jump trap) is marketed, and for certain types of fur it has the same advantages today as it did a hundred years ago. The coilspring trap is also marketed, and for all practical purposes, can be used in any instance where the underspring trap might be used.

Steel traps that are marketed today are made in a variety of sizes. The No. 0, for instance, is a very small trap intended for the trapping of gophers and rats. With a jaw spread of 3½ inches, it will sometimes take larger game but cannot always hold them. The No. 1 trap is ½ inch wider in the jaw spread and is stronger. It will take and hold muskrat, mink, marten, fisher, and weasel. The No. 1½ has a jaw spread of 4⅞ inches and is stronger yet. It will take woodchuck, raccoon, fox, and skunk. A No. 2 will take fox, bobcat, and some coyote. It has two springs instead of one, as the No. 1½ has, and is much stronger. A No. 4 is a wolf trap and would be used also for large coyotes. It might also be used to take mountain lion. The No. 3 is mainly a coyote trap. It will take lynx and even some small wolves.

Some trappers use a killer trap that instantly executes the caught animal. The best-known of this type is the Conibear, named for its inventor and first marketed in the 1950s. It has two wide steel squares that are spring-activated. When the trigger is

This red fox looks sheepish. Most fox are too smart to be taken in such a large and visible trap. *(Photo: Havahart)*

released, the jaws come together with a crushing force that kills the animal either on impact or within a few minutes by preventing it from breathing. Water trappers use this trap most often, but it is also used for dry-land animals, particularly the smaller ones. The Conibear has a number of drawbacks. It is larger than other steel traps and is difficult to hide. It costs more money than a comparable-size steel trap. It is nonselective: With other types, if the trapper catches a nontarget animal such as a dog or a cat he has the option of releasing the animal, usually unhurt, but the killer trap kills a dog as quickly as it does a coyote. In the larger sizes the killer trap has the capability of catching and killing a small child.

Some trappers use some form of live trap to take a problem animal in an area where they do not want to use a steel or a killer trap. These traps are for the most part bulky, and they are expensive. They are difficult to hide and cannot be depended upon to take any quantity of fur. They can be bought from a number of manufacturers, or they can be built. The old familiar box trap is a variation of the live trap. It consists of an enclosure, either wire or wood, and a swinging gate. The gate is held open with a stick or a string attached to the trigger. When the baited trigger is disturbed, the gate releases and the animal is caught.

All of the modern traps are a recent addition to a long line of mechanical devices that have been used to take wildlife for many hundreds of years. Primitive man used equally primitive traps as a major tool to take food and material for clothing. Nets, nooses,

Opposite: A striped skunk is not sure how to get at the bait contained in this Havahart live trap. It smells the bait from the side, goes over the top, and finally, enters and springs the door. *(Photos: Havahart)*

pitfalls, fences, snares, and deadfalls were almost made obsolete when the steel trap was perfected, though the snare and the deadfall are still in limited use.

A deadfall trap consists of a weight that is suspended above a bait. The weight might be a log, a rock, or a plank of wood weighted with a rock. When the bait is disturbed, the trigger releases the weight and it falls on the target, crushing it and usually making an immediate kill. A deadfall will take fur, but it is time-consuming to build. Again, it has the defect of nonselectivity. Targets and nontargets will be killed.

Snares also have occasional use on the trapline. They are cheap to buy and light to carry. At times they will take an educated animal that has lost a toe or two to steel traps and developed an allergy to steel. Most of the time, however, the snare will not take one-tenth of the total fur that a steel trap will. It takes more time to set them and they can be used only in certain applications. Too, the snare is a type of killer trap; any nontarget animal that sticks its head in the noose will be a goner.

The snare is nothing more than a noose of line or fine wire that is suspended in a place where an animal is likely to pass. The snare is used on a trail, on a path through the brush, or at a location where bait is laid to attract the animal. The animal places its head through the suspended noose, and as the bottom of the noose hits its throat, it lunges to get free. The lunging and struggling tighten the noose and the animal soon suffocates.

Poison is sometimes used as a predator-control tool, but it is of little use to the trapper after fur. First, there is the problem of nonselectivity. Second, the animal dies very quickly, and in some parts of the country, will begin to spoil before the trapper arrives to collect the fur. Predators, especially, have very strong stomach acids. With a full belly and a little bit of warm weather, the inside of the skin along the stomach will begin to turn green in a matter of hours. As this tainting progresses it will leave a bad odor to the hide. If it goes far enough it will cause the hair along the area to slip. The area that turns green will darken to an ugly black as the hide dries. Most fur buyers will spot this immediately and will not take the pelt as a gift.

3
Other
Trapping Equipment

The main tool of the trapper, of course, is the trap. Certain other equipment makes the job of trapping much easier. To start with the obvious, the trapper must conceal the trap from the target animal, and unless a water set is being used, that means digging a hole in the ground. A hand pick, a trowel, or a small spade all do a good job of digging a trap cavity. If the ground is hard or rocky, or both, a standard rock hammer, with a pick point on one side, can be very useful.

KNEELING TARP
Certain furbearers are more particular about human scent than others. Both the red fox and the coyote are picky about how the trap site smells. Each loves such smells as carrion and rotten fish oil, but become suspicious of a trap site that smells strongly of a human presence. For that reason a kneeling tarp should be used when setting a trap for these two species. There is no data to support the use of kneeling tarps on other species, but it seems likely that a trap-wise individual of any species might eventually learn to connect the human smell with a trap. Many trappers would rather be safe than sorry and use a kneeling tarp in the making of any set.

A heavy grade of canvas should be used for the kneeling tarp. It should measure about 2 feet by 4 feet. A scrap from an old tent or tarp will do fine. It should be washed thoroughly before it is used. Many such tarps have been treated with a waterproofer that smells strongly of oil. Run the kneeling tarp through the washing machine before using it on the trapline. Check to make sure that all petroleum odor has been removed, and also all odor of the soap or detergent used in the washer. Hang the tarp out to dry over the limb of a tree and allow it to soak up the smells from the woods for several days. When it is dry, fold it carefully and store it in your trap pack. When using the tarp, always put the same side to the ground and the same side up. Otherwise, obviously, the human side would contaminate the trap site about as badly as the trapper's knees would.

TRAP-PAN COVERS

When the trap has been placed in the cavity dug to conceal it, some device must be placed over the trap to prevent dirt from sifting down under the trap pan. The jaws of the trap close when the trap pan is depressed and the pan dog is released. If there is dirt under the pan, it cannot be depressed and the trap will not spring. A large tree leaf can be used for a trap-pan cover if no other material is available.

Many trappers use canvas or denim for pan covers. These must be made odor-free before use, like the kneeling tarp. They will do a good job most of the time, but they do create two problems for the trapper. First, in cold weather the cloth may become wet and then freeze. When it is frozen it will not allow the trap to be sprung. Second, if there are small rodents—squirrels, packrats, mice, chipmunks—in the area, these critters will sniff out the trap location and steal the cloth. They may carry it home for use in nest-building activities, or they may munch on it as a snack. In either case the trap is left with the bare steel exposed.

Ordinary wax paper from the kitchen does a good job as a pan cover. It will not freeze, it is easy to prepare, it is cheap, and it has no odor. Best of all, rodents are not attracted to the wax paper as they are to cloth.

To prepare either cloth or paper pan covers, measure the spread of the jaws of the trap to be used. Cut the paper or the cloth a little bit larger than the open jaw dimensions. It will be better if the wax paper is doubled before it is cut, as the double thickness provides some protection in case of rainy weather and is less likely to collapse from the weight of dirt above. Either cloth or wax-paper pan covers must be protected from odor contamination after they are cut. Use a plastic bag to hold them and then place them in the pack basket.

The trap cover can be used over the pan in two ways. Either

will be effective. The cloth or the wax paper can be laid across the set trap and the edges tucked down under the inside of the trap jaws. If this is done, a slit must be cut in the center of one edge of the cover so that it will fit down over the pan dog. Some trappers simply place the pan cover over the set trap and cover it with dirt. Both techniques have been used by the authors, and both work.

If the pan cover is to be tucked, use a stick to poke the edges of the cover down under the jaws. Some trappers use the index finger of the right hand for this procedure. Those who do can be recognized immediately by the black-and-blue marks left on the finger by the accidentally sprung trap.

WIRE ON THE TRAPLINE

Annealed, or soft, iron wire is useful for many jobs on the trapline. It is often used to wire a trap-chain ring to a drag or a stake. It can be used to tie down to a rock or a tree, or to wire the two chain rings together on a double trap set. Wire is a good friend to have on the trapline but it has to be watched closely to keep it honest. The wire hardens as it is bent and twisted, and trapped animals do a lot of twisting. You should visually inspect all wire stress points after every catch, and replace any wire that appears stressed or kinked. At the end of the trapping year, remove all wire connections and use fresh wire for the next season's trapping. Wire is cheap, and it's better to pay its small price than to lose a valuable furbearer.

SIDECUTTERS

A good heavy-duty pair of sidecutters is almost a necessity on any trapline. The flat jaws will be used many times a day to twist wire onto trap rings, to secure the wired trap to a stake or a drag, and to connect two-trap sets. Get the jumbo size instead of the small pair usually found in the tool box. The big ones will last longer and will be easier to hold onto when your hands are numb and cold from water or wind. The sidecutters will also be used to cut the wire when the traps are removed. Finally, if you use wood stretchers in the drying of the pelt, you'll need small nails to hold the pelt in position on the board. The sidecutters will be handy in removing these tacks when the pelt is taken off the board for turning, and when the pelt is removed permanently from the stretcher.

GLOVES

Rubber gloves are also needed. Some good trappers claim they never use gloves on the trapline, even for the super spookies such as the coyote or red fox. Most money trappers who use the gloves, however, are firm in their belief that the human scent alarms both the coyote and red fox, and also individuals of other species that may have become trap-shy. It is better to be safe than sorry when it comes to fur trapping. Buy the rubber-coated gloves available at most hardware stores, or buy from a trapping-supply house. Such gloves are inexpensive, and the taking of even one bonus fur because of their use will pay the purchase price many times.

DIRT STRAINER

When the trap is in position and the pan cover has been placed, the trap is ready to be covered. If raw dirt were used it is likely that chunks of gravel and sticks would go with the dirt to the top of the trap jaws. Even a pea-sized chunk of gravel could lodge between the jaws of the trap and cause a malfunction. A dirt strainer or sifter screens out these bits of gravel and sticks so that the jaws can close without interference. Many trapping suppliers offer ready-made dirt strainers at a reasonable price. Often these strainers will not meet the specific needs of the individual trapper and he will find it more convenient to build his own. Complete instructions for the construction of a dirt strainer are given in the next chapter.

TRAP STAKES

Trap stakes are used as anchors for the traps. They are used when the trapper wishes to completely hide the set, when no natural tiedowns such as rocks or trees are available, and when the trapper does not wish to use a drag that will allow the animal to pull the trap away from the set. Stakes can also be bought from equipment suppliers at a moderate cost—maybe cheaper than they can be made at home if it is necessary to buy the components. They are, however, made to fit a variety of soil conditions and may not be exactly what is needed for the soil in your area. The construction of trap stakes is fully discussed in Chapter 5.

TRAP DRAGS

A drag is an object attached to the trap that will allow the animal to pull the trap and the drag away from the set. Most of the time the animal will not go far, perhaps only to the nearest clump of heavy brush. A drag is appropriate when the trapper does not want the animal to remain at the set site and tear it up needlessly, when the trap set is exposed to passersby and the trap and the animal are likely to be stolen, and when the trap site is visible from roadways and trails and might offend the sensibilities of nontrappers.

A natural drag such as a tree limb or a rock can often be used. There will be times, however, when no such natural drag is available. There will be other instances when the trapper wishes to hide all evidence of the set. A compact drag made of melted lead is discussed in Chapter 5.

A grapple is a form of drag, allowing the trapped animal to pull away from the trap site. The grapple is a large fishhook-shaped piece of metal that leaves a mark in the ground as it is dragged away. Most trapped animals will seek the protection of a brushy area as they leave the set, and the hooks of the grapple will become caught in the brush. The animal will be hidden and immobilized. Grapples can either be bought or made. There is little difference in the product either way. If the trapper is handy with an acetylene torch and has a quantity of rebar (construction rod) or other metal rod in his junk pile, he can make his own grapples with no investment other than a small quantity of gas and his time.

FUR STRETCHERS

Some trappers take their skinned pelts directly to the deep-freeze. When the fur buyer makes his rounds he buys the frozen skins and the trapper does not bother himself with the fleshing and stretching of the furs. Most of the time, however, the fur buyer expects the fur to be properly fleshed and stretched.

There are two general types of fur stretcher available, the wire stretcher and the wood stretcher. Many trappers use wire stretchers exclusively. They find them low in price, easy to use, and efficient in their function. Other trappers, and probably most of the money trappers, prefer wood stretchers. The wood stretcher takes a bit more time to use, but it has the advantage of being adjustable to permit an exact fit for the fur being stretched. There is a wide variation in size among individual pelts, even those from the same species, and the use of wood stretchers allows the trapper to get the most out of the pelt in the way of length and width. The fur buyer pays on a sliding scale based on length and width, and the trapper who uses wood stretchers correctly will get more for his pelts. Both of the authors prefer to use the wood stretcher. The next chapter discusses stretchers further.

SCENTS

Furbearers are attracted to the trap in only three ways: a scent, a lure, or a bait. There are, of course, also the accidental sets—the ones blind-set in a trail or in the water to catch the animal as it passes. In the strict sense, however, these animals are not brought to the trap; the trap just happens to be where they are walking.

A scent is made from organs or secretions which trigger the animal's mating or territorial instincts. Urine is a scent. Coyote urine, for example, is associated with the animal's concept of his home range. When he smells the urine of a strange coyote in his territory he has a compulsion to deposit urine at the same spot.

A lure is a preparation made from musks, oils, and flesh to stimulate the target animal's curiosity. Many times a lure will be used in conjunction with bait at a trap set. The lure calls the animal to the trap site, and the bait induces the animal to put its foot in the trap. A bait is, of course, a meat or vegetable that is attractive to the animal as a food.

Both scents and lures are easy to make if you have the right ingredients. Mostly it is a simple matter of combining ingredients and letting them age. Most trappers do not use enough scent during a season to warrant the expense of making their own. The same goes for lures. Professional scent and lure makers offer their products at a reasonable price, and the trapper who uses small amounts of each will be time and money ahead if he uses the commercial preparation. Fish oil might be an exception. It is easy to prepare and the ingredients are inexpensive. Chunk bait is another item the trapper should consider making at home. Again, it takes only meat and the action of about three months of summer sun, and it will keep from season to season. Formulas for scents, lures, and baits will be found in the next chapter.

Urine is also available through the trappers' supply houses. The price may seem high, about $25 a gallon, but the alternative may not be appealing. Trappers who collect their own urine trap a coyote prior to the start of the trapping season and pen it up for about a month. A galvanized tin or a plastic floor is placed in the cage and the animal's urine is allowed to flow into a trough that connects to a tank. One coyote would probably pass enough urine in a month's time to last the season. It is a bother, and in some states the keeping of a wild animal is against the law. It is not surprising that most trappers buy their urine from the suppliers.

SKINNING KNIFE

A trapper's knife can be his best friend or his worst enemy. It must have the correct blade shape and heft, and it must accept and hold a razor edge. Any knife will do the job of skinning, and will do a passable job, when it comes right down to it. A knife that is not specifically designed for the skinning of furbearers, though, makes the job harder than it has to be and usually makes it take longer. A good fur-skinning knife should be small. All of the skinning is done with the last ½ inch of the blade, so a big-bladed knife is not needed. Too, a big-bladed knife is heavy. You might not notice it on the first coyote, but you surely will after skinning two or three in a row. The end of the blade should have a slight upcurve on the cutting side.

Generally speaking, there are two types of knife steel. One is a highly tempered steel which sharpens slowly but holds its edge well. The other is a softer steel that permits fast sharpening. The soft steel, of course, does not hold the edge as long as the hard steel, and will require more frequent sharpening. The type used depends on personal preference.

Any knife is only as good as the device used to keep it sharp. Most hunters and trappers are familiar with the Carborundum stone. It does a good job. The Arkansas stone (novaculite) does a better job but costs more. If you have not tried the new line of sharpening steels offered by Gerber or Shrade, now might be a good time. They put a good edge on a knife super-fast. One or two licks on each side of the blade usually does the trick. They seem to do as good a job as the best stone, and they are much faster. Anything that saves you time means more money when payday arrives.

BINOCULARS

Binoculars are not an absolute necessity on a trapline. A good pair, however, can save you a lot of extra steps if you use them correctly. The new roof-prism binoculars offered by Bushnell and Pentax are good, and if you have a really fat wallet, the Leitz Trinovid is great. The glasses should be compact and no heavier than necessary. They will often be carried in the pack, and with the other equipment that a trapper must carry, weight soon becomes a problem. The glasses should be of good optical quality to prevent eyestrain.

Binoculars are used to scout country to determine locations for trap sets and to check traps across canyons to see if they hold furbearers. It might take only seconds to check a trap with the glasses when it would take an hour or more to cover the distance on foot.

FIREARM

A small-caliber handgun or rifle is also needed. A pistol or revolver is the best bet, as it is light and will fit in a belt holster. Many individuals, however, cannot hit the side of a barn with a handgun even if they are inside and shooting out. For those, a handgun would be a poor choice. Better to stick with a rifle. Whether you choose a handgun or rifle, get the model that will shoot either the .22 Short or the .22 Long Rifle cartridge. The .22 CB (conical bullet) is a very low-power cartridge that is suitable for smaller animals, but is sometimes hard to find. The .22 Short is universally available and will not damage pelts if the shot is carefully placed.

A skunk in a trap can be killed with a stick, but it soon turns into a messy business, and your wife might ask you to sleep in the garage when you get home. A .22 Short, however, placed behind the skunk's shoulder, does the dirty deed with no muss or fuss, and leaves a very small hole. The gun will also be used to shoot bait for bait sets.

You should shoot any trapped animal that is not securely caught. Many times a trapper tries to use the kill stick on a coyote or bobcat that is held only by a toe or two. Usually he is treated to the dismal sight of a furry rear end disappearing over the horizon. At the first swing the critter makes a lunge and pulls loose, and then hotfoots it out of sight. It is better to shoot these marginally held animals. Use the .22 Short, again, and try to put the little bullet at the center of an X drawn between the eyes and the ears. There will be a very small hole to repair and almost no blood to stain the fur. The escape of one bobcat due to kill pullout will lose the trapper enough money to pay for a couple of guns.

KILL STICK

A kill stick is a device to knock out the trapped animal so that it can be safely dispatched. It can be wood or metal and should be about 4 feet long. The handle of a golf putter is about right. Use a hacksaw to cut off the metal head. Strike with the padded end of the shaft, as it will be less likely to cut the hide and cause bleeding. One medium tap between the eyes is usually enough. This will put the animal down and out and will give you a chance to bring your foot down forcefully on the critter's chest behind the front leg. A couple of these licks will usually collapse the lungs and the animal will die from internal bleeding. If done correctly this is humane and fast, and moreover there will be no external blood to stain the pelt.

TOPOGRAPHY MAPS

Topography, or topo, maps can be an aid in setting up a trapline if you use them to best advantage. Most such maps show elevation changes, usually in increments of 20 feet, and major topographic features such as rivers, streams, lakes, trails, roads, cabins, and mines. Many also show major vegetational changes. The maps can tell the trapper the most likely habitat for the furbearing species, the easiest way to walk into trapping country, and the location of major visible landmarks which will help to keep him oriented. The maps can be ordered from the U.S. Geological Survey. For areas east of the Mississippi, write Branch of Distribution, U.S.G.S., 1200 South Eads Street, Arlington, Va. 22202; for areas west of the Mississippi, write Branch of Distribution, U.S.G.S., Box 25286 Federal Center, Denver, Colo. 80225. Either place will send a folder describing the topo-map symbols and a list of maps available. There is a modest charge for the maps.

4
Getting Ready

The summer months, when there is no trapping, is the time to do the maintenance work on the traps and other trapping equipment. If the trapper has the time he can also use the summer to make many of the items of equipment that he will need.

TRAP MAINTENANCE

All used traps should be checked to discover any defective parts. Like any other item of mechanical equipment, traps will fail occasionally. The inspection will be more efficient if a routine is followed. Start with the trap chain of each trap and check for broken or stressed links. Check the swivel between the trap and the chain. It should work freely. If the swivel is jammed so that it does not allow the trap to turn without turning the chain, any large animal that is trapped will soon twist out.

Set the traps to check the spring tension. An old trap may have a weak spring and will likely not hold an animal as it should. If one or more springs in a longspring trap are weak they should be repaired or replaced. To repair, remove the spring from the trap and place the inside of the V over a V-shaped piece of wood that is slightly larger than the inside of the trap. Use a hammer to strike the spring and drive it down onto the wood. This will spread the inside of the spring and restore some of its strength. If the spring has been overheated it will not hold new tension. Place these traps and any others that have been damaged beyond repair in the salvage pile. They can be used for parts to repair other less seriously damaged traps.

Use care when removing the springs from a trap with cast jaws. It is necessary to bend the trap bottom and the bottom posts slightly to remove the springs, and the cast jaws will often break if excessive force is used. Do not pound on the cast jaws.

Traps with drawn jaws have more spring and can be bent and

removed from the trap with little risk. Trap springs on the Victor and the Blake & Lamb traps are interchangeable. Usually the Newhouse trap springs can also be interchanged with those from traps of the same size and configuration.

The condition of the trap jaws is also important. Look for cracks or other damage to the jaw tips. Bring the jaws of the trap out to the face of the trap bottom posts. The jaws should protrude through the holes on each end from ⅛ to ¼ inch. When the jaws are closed the tips should be bent slightly upward. If the jaws are of a different height when closed, place the trap on a flat surface and tap the high jaw with a hammer until it is lowered to the other jaw. This will also bring the bottom of the jaw tight against the bottom post holes.

If the jaws are bent so that a gap appears between them when they are closed, lay them flat on an anvil and use a hammer to bring them back into shape. This condition shows up often on the underspring jump trap.

Offset jaws should have a ³/₁₆-inch spread. In the No. 3 and No. 4 traps a center spread of ¼ inch is not unusual. If a ³/₁₆-inch spread is required and the traps are not of the offset type, set the trap and use an electric welder to place a spot bead on the ends of one jaw. The beads should be just above where the upper edge of the spring comes when the trap is closed. If the bead is too large it can be filed slightly until the correct distance is left. If only a few traps must be adjusted a temporary correction can be obtained by wrapping a stiff wire around the inside of one trap jaw until the desired spread is obtained.

A No. 3 or No. 4 longspring trap will have about ³/₁₆-inch offset if one jaw is removed and reversed and then put back on the trap.

When the jaws of a trap are closed there should be an opening between the lower part of the jaws of about ³/₁₆ inch at post level. The opening should taper and disappear at the point where the spring hits. This opening is needed to prevent dirt, the pan cover, or other material from clogging the trap as it is sprung.

If the jaws of the trap close tightly all the way to the bottom post holes and with a ³/₁₆-inch flat face on the jaws, the trap will often close improperly. Underspring jump traps often have this condition. To correct, set the trap and use a file to round the lower striking edge or make it a V shape. This will allow the trap to cut through dirt and sticks that may otherwise clog it. This should be done to the inside of both trap jaws near the bottom ends. The trap will close faster and with more snap. The reworked portion should start at the point where the jaw bottom fits into the trap frame and extend up about an inch.

Check the jaws carefully to find metal burrs or any sharp edges, particularly in the area where the trap springs slide. These imperfections may slow the action of the closing trap and cause the loss of a furbearer. Use a file to smooth off these rough edges so that the trap closes smoothly and with no hesitation.

Set each longspring trap and turn the spring or springs from one side to the other. If the lower part of the spring binds on the bottom post, place a set of vise-grip pliers on the spring to hold it open. Close the trap jaws and file the bottom edges of the posts so that the lower spring ring turns smoothly. The problem may be noticed more often in coilspring traps and under spring jump traps. The bottom posts are often too big for the spring holes of the underspring jump trap and the lever hole of the coilspring trap.

To adjust the coilspring trap, push down on the lever or levers until the jaws open enough to set the trap. If the lever scrapes the bottom posts or binds, close the jaws and let the levers up. File the edges of the bottom posts until they are rounded and smooth. The trap will now be easier to set and it will spring faster.

The underspring jump trap should be checked for spring-hole clearance on the bottom post edges. Push the spring down and set the trap. If there is contact with the bottom post that creates friction, the trap action will be slowed. File post edges until a smooth action is obtained.

The pan of a trap, even a new trap, must usually be adjusted to obtain maximum efficiency. Check the pan to make sure that it is solid on the shank. If the pan is loose it can be tightened by welding or riveting. Place the trap shank on an anvil or other metal surface and use a ball-peen hammer to rivet the shank part that protrudes through the pan.

The shank should also be properly fastened to the cross. If this is in good shape, some adjustment is then needed to prepare the shank groove for the dog. Use a 6-inch flat file to shape the part that the end of the dog is against. It should be perfectly flat. Often, too much pan depression is needed to cause the trap to spring. A furbearer may feel the sinking action of the pan and draw out its foot before the trap closes, causing a miss, or a catch that is held only by a toe or two. If this condition exists, file the pan-dog groove until the springing distance is shortened.

To put the pan dog into proper shape, file the end until it is square and with a slight taper to the rear. This will permit a fast close and will take furbearers that would otherwise pull away. The pan height, when the trap is set, should be level with the jaws. If the pan is too high, the catch will likely be low on the foot. A high catch is better, as it grabs more of the leg. To raise pan height, use pliers and a large crescent wrench to bend the raised part of the cross backward. Lower the pan by bending the cross forward. The trap should spring when the pan is depressed midway between the jaw level and the cross.

If new traps have excessive spring tension, the spring can be totally compressed and wired in that position for several months. This will keep the trap from breaking the bone of the animal's leg. Most traps lose this excessive strength after they are used for a year or so.

Marking for Identification

If the traps are new and have not been marked with your identifying number or name, this is the next step. Many states require that traps be so marked as an aid to enforcement officers who may have occasion to contact the trapper. Trap thieves are less likely to steal a trap that is properly marked, and if a trap is stolen, the owner has a better chance of recovery if the trap is marked. Too, to successfully prosecute the thief, the owner must be able to identify his property positively. Sometimes traps are lost when a furbearer pulls a stake or breaks a tiedown wire. If the trap is marked the owner has a better chance of recovery if it is found by a third party.

The best method of marking traps is with a steel stamp to imprint a number or a series of letters directly into the metal of the trap. Do not stamp the trap on a part that can be easily replaced. Stamp on the frame if possible, and in more than one place. To stamp, place the trap on an anvil or a solid piece of wood. Do not attempt to imprint the stamp on the trap springs. Some states require that each trap have a metal tag attached showing the name and the address of the trapper. These tags are available from a number of trap suppliers. They do little, however, to prevent theft. The thief can readily remove them and substitute his own tags. Steel tags are a better bet than the aluminum; large predators may chew off aluminum tags.

Cleaning

After maintenance and marking, the traps are ready to be cleaned. If they are new they should be washed in soapy water to remove the oil and grease. Then they should be placed in a safe location to weather until they have taken on an even coat of rust. Traps that have never been rusted will not take dye and wax as readily as rusted traps. In the Southwest, where rain is infrequent, it may be necessary to spray the traps with a garden hose occasionally to speed the rusting. This may take several weeks.

When the traps have acquired an even coat of rust they are ready for derusting. To derust, the traps are boiled in a lye solution. If you have a lot of traps a 55-gallon steel drum makes a good container. If the drum is to be used upright, the top third of the barrel may be removed for easier handling. The drum may also be used on its side, first cutting off the top third of the long portion. This permits a larger area of the metal to come in contact with the fire. If you have only a few traps to be treated you can use a smaller container, perhaps a 5-gallon can or pail.

The container should be positioned on flat rocks or cement blocks above the firepit. Leave about 12 to 16 inches between the bottom of the firepit and the bottom of the container. This will accept enough wood so that a hot fire can be built. Place the traps in the container and fill with water until all traps are covered. Add about four cans of lye for the 55-gallon drum. Be careful not to splash lye water on your hands or clothing. If you do, flush it off immediately with clean water.

Boil the traps in the lye water until all are clean. This will take about half an hour. When the traps are clean, remove them with a metal hook and place them on a screen away from the fire to drain. Do not let the smoke from the fire blow on the traps, as it will give them a smoke odor. Rinse the cleaned traps with a hose to remove all traces of the lye water. Continue the process until all traps have been derusted. Empty the container of the lye water and rinse well with fresh water.

Dyeing

The cleaned traps are now ready for dyeing. The dye turns the trap a dark color and prevents rusting while they are on the line. Use 1 pound of logwood crystals for each 5 gallons of water. If the cut 55-gallon drum is used, fifty or sixty traps can be treated at a time.

Bring the logwood solution to a boil and boil the traps for at least thirty minutes. Then check to determine the color. Continue boiling until all of the traps have accepted a uniform dark-gray color. When sufficiently darkened, remove the traps from the solution with a wire hook and place them on wire mesh to dry. Continue until all traps have been dyed.

Logwood chips are available from most trappers' suppliers at a moderate cost. Black-walnut hulls are also effective for dyeing traps. Use 1 gallon of hulls for each 5 gallons of water and follow the same procedure used with the logwood crystals. For a very dark color, bring the solution to a boil and leave the traps in the water for eight hours. Let the fire burn down after a boil is reached. When all traps have been dyed, empty the water from the barrel and rinse it with clean water.

Waxing

The cleaned and dyed traps are now ready for waxing. Prepare all traps by placing a nail between the trap jaws so that the jaws will be slightly open and the wax can reach the inside of the jaws. Prepared trap wax is available from the suppliers, and it does a good job, but you may want to make your own. First, clean pure beeswax by boiling it in the container. Again, the container size will be determined by the amount of wax to be processed. Fill the container two-thirds full of water and bring to a boil, with the wax melting on the surface. Skim any foreign material or scum from the surface of the melted wax. Let the water and the wax boil for half an hour or more, and then remove it from the heat and allow it to cool. The beeswax will form a crust on top of the water. Put the wax layers on wax paper or aluminum foil and place it in the sun.

The wax can be used as it is or it can be mixed with paraffin. Use 4 pounds of paraffin to 1 pound of beeswax to obtain a mix that will work well as a trap wax. If you are trapping in an area where there are pine trees, a good trap wax can be made by adding ¼ pound of pine sap or pine resin to the paraffin-beeswax mixture. This gives the traps a faint piny odor.

To wax the traps, use a 5-gallon container two-thirds filled with water and with 2 pounds of the prepared wax added. This is enough for all of the traps used on a small trapline. If you have a long line and several hundred traps to be waxed, use a larger container, such as the cut-down 55-gallon drum, with about 30 gallons of water and 6 to 12 pounds of the prepared wax. This will coat at least 200 traps of the size used for most of the larger predators, such as cat and coyote.

Get the water hot enough so the wax liquefies. Put two traps together, and using an S-shaped hook 10 to 12 inches long, lower the traps into the water. Hook the upper end of the S hook on the barrel edge and leave them in the water until they have had time to heat to water temperature. Continue adding traps to the water until eight or ten pairs are submerged. Remove them, slowly bringing them up through the layer of melted wax and letting the excess wax drip from the traps back into the barrel. Place the waxed traps on wire mesh to dry. The trap chains should also be exposed to the waxing. Keep at it until all traps and chains have been waxed. Do not handle the traps or the chains with the bare hands after the waxing has been completed; use rubber gloves or metal hooks.

When all traps and chains are waxed it is time to give the same treatment to all drags, grapples, and stakes. Handle these also with rubber gloves or metal hooks after waxing. The waxed traps, chains, drags, grapples, and stakes should be stored in the open air, safe from human or animal contamination.

You may have to repeat the whole process in midseason because of wax wearoff from caught animals. Usually one rewaxing session is enough each season.

You may find that the wax flakes from the treated traps. This can be eliminated by waxing the traps in pure wax with no water. Melt 2 gallons of the pure paraffin-beeswax mixture in a 5-gallon can. Wax two traps at a time if using either No. 3 or No. 4 traps. Smaller traps can be waxed four to six at a time. This system is slower than the water-wax method, but does a superior job of waxing.

The wax is very flammable; care must be taken to prevent it from catching fire. Traps that are warm before they are lowered into the wax will accept the wax more readily and more evenly. The traps should be completely dry if waxing by the pure-wax method.

STRETCHERS

The skins of furbearers are prepared for sale in one of two ways: open and cased. Most of the skins are presented cased, or tube-skinned. When animals are skinned in this manner the trapper must have a way to allow the pelt to dry to the proper dimension with no wrinkling or shrinking. The drying board, or stretcher, serves this purpose.

There are three general types of drying boards, and each will do the job if properly used. Most fur suppliers offer wire stretchers in sizes to fit most furbearers. Many trappers, as has been mentioned, object to the wire stretcher for larger furbearers because it stretches all skins to a standard size. The smaller furs of a species may overstretch a bit, and the larger ones may not stretch to their full potential. Most trappers use one of the two remaining types.

Both of the other types of drying boards are made of wood. One is made from a solid piece of wood and is carved in sizes to fit the variations in a species, and the other is constructed of two pieces of wood with an air space between. The latter type is adjustable to compensate for variations in individuals. The two-piece dryer is recommended for furbearers of fox size and larger.

To make a two-piece stretcher that will accommodate a coyote, start with a 1 x 6 piece of pine that is at least 6 feet in length. Rip the piece down the center by using a table saw. If none is available, have the piece ripped at the lumber yard. The yield will be two 6-foot pieces each about 2¾ inches wide. Taper one end of each piece to obtain a taper that closely resembles the taper in the nose of a coyote. Sand the taper smooth. Now drive a small nail into the inside tip of the tapered end about an inch. Pull the nail out with a pair of pliers and drive it into the corresponding spot on the opposite board. Cut the nail head off with a pair of sidecutters and put the two boards together. Cut one more piece of the 1-inch stock to serve as a crosspiece for the stretcher. When the hide is placed on the stretcher and tacked into position, the two legs can be separated at the wide end until the desired tension is achieved. The board is then secured in this position by nailing the crosspiece to each of the legs.

Some trappers use bolts instead of nails in the crosspiece. Drill a hole and bolt the crosspiece to one of the legs. Cut a slot in the other end of the crosspiece and run a bolt through this slot and through a hole in the opposite leg. Attach a thumbscrew and the crosspiece can be tightened in position.

The length and width of the stretcher will depend on the animal for which it is intended. Average dimensions for furbear-

The point of the stretcher can be fitted with a headless nail to prevent slippage.

ers that are case-skinned are listed on page 34 (tail not included) in inches.

It should be remembered that the sizes given are rough averages. Many of the species have a wide size variation in different parts of their range, and what may be an average pelt in one area may be a large one in another. But these measurements will give you a starting point in the construction of your drying boards, and you can then adjust the dimensions to meet the size of the pelts in your particular trapping area.

It should also be noted that fur buyers grade the fur on a number of factors, and one of those factors is size. A properly stretched fur will allow the fur buyer to pay the top price that the grade of fur allows. Care here can earn the trapper many extra dollars during the course of a season. More information on correct drying size will be offered in the chapters dealing with specific animals.

A coyote stretched on a homemade wood-leg stretcher. The bottom crosspiece is nailed or bolted into position to supply tension. The legs, hips, and nose are nailed into position before the crosspiece is tightened. *(Photos: Gerry Blair)*

SPECIES	Length	Hips	Shoulders
Badger	28	10	9
Bobcat	33	9	7.5
Coyote	50	12	9.5
Fisher	32	7	6
Red fox	28	7	5.5
Gray fox	24	7	5.5
Lynx	34	9	7.5
Marten	17	4	3
Mink	23	3.75	3
Muskrat	15	6.5	5
Opossum	19	6	5.5
Otter	50	7.5	6
Raccoon	24	9	6.5
Ringtail cat	18	4	3
Skunk	21	8	6
Spotted skunk	15	5.5	4.5
Weasel	13	2	1.5
Wolf	66	13	11

HOMEMADE LURES, BAIT, AND SCENT

Fish oil, when correctly prepared, can be used to call most predatory animals. Fox, coyote, bobcat, and skunk find it attractive. So do badger, raccoon, and mink. A fatty type of fish does the best job; carp is good, and so is catfish.

To prepare the oil, cut the fish into 1-inch chunks and place them in a gallon jar. Use heavy glass or crockery, never metal. Lay a piece of flat glass over the top of the jar and put a weight on top of the glass. This will hold the glass tight against the jar and prevent flies from laying their eggs on the fish. Gases will form as the solids break down, and as the pressure builds up the glass cover will be slightly lifted to let the gas escape. Put the jar in the summer sun in a place that is safe from cats and dogs.

As the fish rots, the oil will appear on the surface. Let the mixture keep working for a period of several weeks. After a period of time, an amber liquid will appear above the solids. Pour this oil into a clean bottle and replace the lid. The mixture will keep working and will produce more oil as the summer progresses.

Chunk bait is another item the trapper can prepare at home

Fish-oil lure in the making. The glass cover keeps blowflies out, but allows pressure to escape. *(Photo: Gerry Blair)*

with a minimum investment. If done right the product will equal or exceed the quality of the chunk baits offered by commercial suppliers.

Chunk bait is made in a manner similar to fish oil. Use any meat for the bait. Chunks cut from the backstrap and the loins of a coyote, fox, or bobcat will work fine. If they are not available use old venison or other meat from the freezer. Cut the meat into 1-inch cubes and put it in a glass or crockery container. Again, cover the top of the container with a weighted sheet of glass to prevent contamination by flies. Let the material sit in the summer sun in a place safe from dogs and cats until the meat begins to break down, about three or four weeks. Add borax to the meat to prevent further spoilage. If you're going to use the bait in subfreezing areas, it might be well to add a bit of glycerine to the preparation to prevent freezing.

If you want to make your own scent the following will take most varieties of predators. Use the anal glands from a fox or a coyote, the glands from the flex part of the rear legs, and the dark glands from just below the ear. Add to this the last 6 inches of the intestine, along with any fecal material enclosed. Add the bladder and about ¼ pound of liver with the bile attached. Add ¼ pound of brain. Let all this sit and age for one or two years, protected from blowfly contamination. If available, the reproductive organs from a female coyote or fox will make the scent better. Some trappers let the material age and then add the urine from a bobcat to produce a watery consistency.

OTHER EQUIPMENT
There are a number of other items that the trapper will need in running the trapline or caring for the pelts. All of the equipment is available commercially, and if you are short of time and long on money you will find it more convenient to buy the items. For those who are handy, however, and who want to save money, here are directions for making the items.

Fleshing Board and Flesher
A fleshing board is a solid board that is roughly the shape of the stretched animal skin. It holds the green pelt so that the trapper can remove the excess flesh and fat. The board should be of 1-inch pine stock. Cut the board to the rough dimensions of the pelt to be fleshed.

A fleshing board can be made that will accept most sizes of pelts. Use a pine 2 x 4 that is free of knots. Taper the end and the sides and sand smooth. Use a 5-foot length if most of your catch is the large predators, and a smaller length if most is the smaller animals.

Any dull scraping instrument can be modified to serve as a flesher. An old putty knife does a good job. Get the type with the wide blade, about 3 inches, and sand or file off the sharp edges on the blade end and the corners. A larger knife can be made from any piece of scrap iron or steel. Make it long enough so that it is comfortable to handle. Wood handles on the ends make it handy to use. Some trappers use only a large tablespoon to do their fleshing. The spoon should be of the heavy steel type; otherwise it will soon bend and break from the constant pressure.

Dirt Strainer
A dirt strainer is a simple item to make; any trapper can make a serviceable strainer in less than one hour. Buy a piece of ¼-inch-mesh hardware cloth in the size of the intended strainer. A

piece 1 foot square will be plenty big. If you intend to run a line using a vehicle, you might want to make the strainer to the dimensions of the hardware cloth. Build a wood framework a bit smaller than the hardware cloth, of 1-inch-square stock. Butt the ends and nail or screw. Bend the edges of the hardware cloth along the edges of the frame and either nail or staple it into position.

An empty gallon metal can also makes a good dirt strainer. Use one with a handle and leave the handle on. Cut away the top and the bottom of the can. Cut a piece of hardware cloth that is a bit larger than the can bottom and fit it into shape, then soft-solder the hardware cloth into position.

5
Using Drags, Grapples, and Stakes

All traps must be secured in some manner to immobilize the trapped animal, or to confine and restrict its movements, until the trapper arrives. In many trapping activities the trapper may use natural features of the landscape for the tiedown. A tree, a rock, or a bush is often used to secure the trap if it is the trapper's intention to completely immobilize the trapped animal. At other times the tiedown may be used with other natural features to cause the immediate death of the animal and prevent twist-offs. Many water animals, as an example, are trapped so that they will drown soon after they are caught.

DRAGS

A drag is nothing more than a weight attached to the end of the trap chain that allows the animal to move away from the trap set a short distance. The drag must permit some movement, but not so much that the animal will travel a long distance, perhaps escaping, and in any event causing extra work for the trapper.

A drag can be made at the set site using natural materials in many instances. Dead or live limbs from trees will often make effective drags. Rocks can sometimes be used, particularly when the rock is shaped so that it will accept a wiring harness easily. Round rocks are poor choices. Find a rock that is the right size for the area being trapped. In brushy country a rock weighing 10 to 15 pounds would do the job. An oblong rock seems to work best. Use trap wire to make a strong loop about one-third of the way in from each end. Use more wire to cross-wire the two end loops together. This harness will not come loose no matter in what direction the

No matter which way the trapped animal pulls, this wire will not come loose from the rock. *(Photo: Gerry Blair)*

animal pulls. Wire the trap-chain loop to the middle, or crossover, wire. The rock can then be buried beneath the trap or concealed in other ways.

If you use a tree limb as a drag, make a close inspection of the limb to ensure that no weak areas exist that would break under pressure. The animal will likely entangle itself in brush and will then be able to exert a direct hard pull on the drag. Large animals such as coyote, bobcat, badger, and a few others are surprisingly strong. Use a stout limb and make sure it has no rotten or weak areas to break under a direct pull. The tiedown is secured with trapping wire.

There are many possibilities for nonnatural drags. Gears from old farm machinery or automobiles work well. Any item that has weight without undue bulk is satisfactory. A trip to any farm junkpile should provide a number of candidates. Some trappers make a very efficient drag by melting scrap lead into a can about the size of a beer can. Cut away the top so that the melted lead can be poured in easily. Lead is easily melted with a plumber's torch or even on top of the stove. Have a loop of metal ready to place in the end of the poured weight. This will make it easier to hook the trap chain to the weight. Such a weight is heavy for its size and can easily be hidden, and either alone or in partnership with a grapple will leave a trail for the trapper to follow.

GRAPPLES

A grapple is a type of drag. To select a grapple the trapper must consider the country to be trapped. A grapple that would work well in very brushy country might not do the job on the open desert.

The old standby grapple, the one most often used by trappers, is the double hook on a 4-foot chain. If the traps being used have a short chain, rigged for stakes, a 5-foot chain on the grapple is better. To make a grapple, use $5/16$-inch or $3/8$-inch rod. The construction rod called rebar does a good job and can often be had at no cost around construction projects. Ask the foreman if you can haul away the scrap rebar when the job is finished. The shaft of the grapple should be about 8 inches long, with two hooks bent out to form a half-circle. The tips of the hooks should be about 3 inches out from the shaft. One grapple requires about 30 inches of rod. The shaft is doubled to make the hooks, and an opening is left at the top of the shaft to accommodate the chain. An S hook placed in the opening makes it handy to attach the chain. A swivel can be put near the S hook, between the chain of the grapple, to prevent kinking. This grapple is easy and cheap to make. It works best in brushy areas, where a caught animal will likely go no farther than 20 or 30 feet before it becomes entangled. If the area is more open it may travel several hundred yards. At times, the trapper will encounter an educated animal that will go farther. Sometimes a coyote will take the grapple in its mouth and travel a mile or more.

The trapper can make it more difficult for the animal to leave the country by using a weight in partnership with the grapple. This combination also works well in open country where the grapple by itself would not be effective. Weld a chain link, or half a chain link, to the bottom of the grapple where the two prongs bend away from each other. Attach a swivel to this link and put on about 10 inches of chain. Bend a $3/16$-inch galvanized wire to form a half-circle, and fill an old beer can with melted lead, using the bent wire as a bail. Attach the bail to the chain coming from the

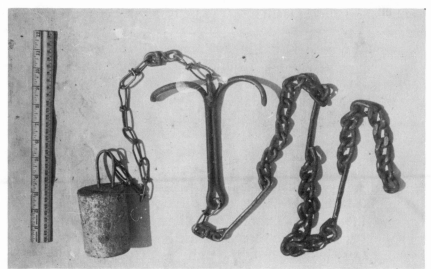

Grapple-weight combination used on the authors' trapline. The lead weight was molded in a 12-ounce can. *(Photo: Bill Musgrove)*

bottom of the grapple. Get the lead from service stations that may have old tire weights around. The lead cores from old car batteries may also be used. This combination works very well. The grapple hangs in the brush, and the lead weight leaves a good track on the ground in open areas. When the caught animal is on a hillside trail, the lead weight has a tendency to roll downhill and let the grapple catch on brush. The grapple-weight combination also makes it difficult for the animal to take the grapple in its mouth and run. The compact size makes the outfit easy to transport and also easy to bury beneath the trap. If two traps are set, bury the grapple and weight under one trap and the chain under the other.

Another grapple often used is the very effective three-prong grapple. With three points instead of two, one of the points is always down to drag the ground. These are a bit more difficult to make than the two-prong grapple. They are also harder to pack and keep separated, and they take more work to hide at the trap site. They are made about the same as the two-prong grapple, except a third shank and hook is made and is welded to the two-pronger.

All chains and grapples should be cleaned, dyed, and waxed in the same way that the traps are, and when they have been treated they should be handled only with rubber gloves. A furbearer can smell bad scent from a grapple just as well as it can from a trap.

When you're handling a large number of grapples, it is better to box them or hang them individually to prevent tangles. It also helps to make three or four loops of the attached chain and use trap wire to maintain the loops.

STAKES

Stakes are used when the trapper wants to immobilize the trapped animal. Stakes do the same job as a natural tiedown. The trapper will find, however, that natural tiedowns are not always available at the place where he wants to set. Too, the use of a stake as a tiedown allows the trapper to hide all evidence of the trap.

Many furbearers are lost because stakes of the wrong size have been used, or stakes of the right size have been used in the wrong way. The diameter and length of the stake should be determined by the type of ground at the trap site and the species of animal the trapper is after. Stakes with a rough surface, such as rebar or large bolts, will have more holding power than smooth ones. To make a stake from a piece of rebar, sharpen one end of the bar to a point so that it will go into the ground easily. Weld a nut onto the other end of the bar to provide a striking surface for the hammer. Cut lengths to 10, 16, and 22 inches. This will give a stake for hard soil, medium soil, and sand.

Power-line companies use a bolt that makes an excellent trap stake. The bolts are galvanized and come in lengths of 10, 12, 14, and 16 inches. They are of ⅝-inch stock. The bolts are not quite long enough for sandy soil, but will work well in either hard or medium ground. Trappers can often find these discarded around areas where old lines are coming down. Others may be found at secondhand stores.

Also good are the bolts used to hold cable spools together. They come in ⅝-inch and ¾-inch diameter and are usually either 30 or 36 inches long. This is longer than the trapper needs, and these bolts should be shortened to 24 inches. If a heating torch is available, the dirt end of the bolt can be flattened to a spade point. Before flattening, put a large washer on the bolt. The flattened end will keep the washer on and it will help to keep the bolt from turning in the hole. A hole should be drilled in the washer edge about halfway between the center hole and the edge to make a

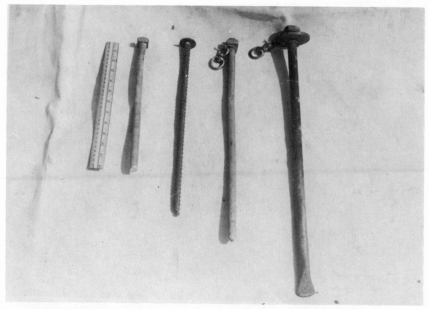

Stakes made from varying lengths of bolts and rebar. *(Photo: Bill Musgrove)*

place for the tie-on. Use a swivel here to minimize the pull on the stake. A short trap chain, 10 to 12 inches, works the best with a stake. Some trappers use a longer chain, however, as they feel that the long chain reduces the pull on the stake and is less likely to be pulled out. On a loose stake the long chain might be an advantage. The short chain will work well on a tight stake. It has the added advantage of preventing the caught animal from taking long jumps against the chain. If these jumps are eliminated the critter is less apt to pull the stake, pull a toe from the trap, or hurt itself.

If the set is a two-trap set, the use of this bolt stake will give the trapper some insurance. If the caught animal pulls the stake it will also pull the second trap. The stake and the second trap will make a good drag, and if the ground is not too hard, will leave a trail for the trapper to follow.

Wooden stakes are still used by trappers in many areas. Hardwood such as oak or hickory is usually picked. Wrap two or three tight turns of trap wire about ¼ inch from the top to keep the stake from splitting and to keep the top edges from breaking off. The stake can be made more effective by placing a series of downward-slanting small cuts on the sides. These stakes are easy

Do not stake a trap for a climbing animal at the foot of a tree. By climbing, the caught animal has a straight up pull and will usually pull out the stake. *(Photo: Norm Woolsey, Arizona Game and Fish Dept.)*

to make, and if they wear out quickly, the trapper does not suffer a great loss.

Both metal and wooden stakes work better if they are fitted with a swivel between the stake and the trap chain. The swivel keeps the chain from balling up on the stake head. Both metal and wooden stakes should be treated before use. Metal stakes get the same treatment as the traps—degreasing, dyeing, and waxing. Wooden stakes should be dyed and waxed.

If the ground is hard or medium-hard, or frozen, the trapper can usually use a shorter stake than he would otherwise. A stake ½ to ¾ inch in diameter and 10 to 12 inches long will do the job on a coyote or anything smaller. In open fields or meadows you'll need a longer stake—16 to 18 inches—because the ground is looser. In loamy or sandy areas such as the bottom of a sand wash, or water-saturated ground, don't use anything less than 20 to 24 inches.

Some care is necessary in the placement of the stake in relation to nearby land features. Do not place stakes at the bottom of a steep bank. The animal will climb the bank and can then pull straight up on the stake. Avoid areas with large rocks nearby for the same reason. If trapping for cat, or if a bobcat is likely to come to the coyote trap, do not stake at the bottom of a tree. The cat will surely climb the tree and have an easy time pulling the stake. And a stake driven too close to the edge of a dirt bank will often pull out if the animal lunges to the weak side.

6
Nontarget Animals

Nontarget animals can be a headache to the trapper. If he is trapping in an area where there are many houses and farms he will likely catch dogs and housecats. While the nontarget animal is in the trap, no furbearer can be caught there. In all likelihood the animal will tear up the set so that it will have to be rebuilt. In releasing the animal, the trapper risks being bitten or scratched for his trouble.

Other nontarget animals plague the trapper. Predatory and scavenging birds will often be caught unless the trapper takes adequate precaution. Small meat-eating birds such as jays will also come to the trap and will be caught. So will all rodents and also rabbits. Big-game animals such as deer and javelina will also be attracted to any set using a meat bait. Most of these nontarget animals can be protected from their curiosity if the trapper makes his sets correctly. The ones that persist can usually be released unharmed with nothing hurt but their dignity.

DOGS

If there are dogs running loose in the area being trapped there is no way they can be kept from the trap if the target animal is of the dog family. A loose-running dog acts much like a fox, coyote, or wolf when it is off by itself or running in a pack. Usually, though, dogs are not as smart as their wild relatives. Dogs will come to bait sets, to sets using lures, and to sets where the only scent is coyote or fox urine. The dog will usually be caught just as the target animal would have been caught, by the low part of one front leg. Unless it is a very small dog there is a good probability that the legbone will not be broken. The trapper should evaluate the caught dog carefully before he decides upon a course of action. If the dog has been caught in an area where the trapper knows there are no houses within miles, and it is his opinion that the dog is feral, or running

This coyote has been taken from the trap using a noose stick. Trappers can use the noose stick to release nontarget and unwanted catches. *(Photo: Gerry Blair)*

wild, the trapper will do the wildlife of the area a favor by destroying the dog. If, on the other hand, the dog is caught near a ranch or farmhouse and the trapper thinks that it is an owned animal, he should release the dog to return home.

Some dogs are as large as wolves and are just as dangerous. Take no chances with a trapped dog. Even if it wags its tail at your approach it may decide to chew off your right arm when you attempt to open the trap to free it. Dogs can be released in two general ways. If the dog is not large, you can throw a coat over the animal's head and hold it down. While the dog is so covered you can open the trap and allow the dog to pull its leg free. Step back without removing the coat and let the dog run out from under it. It will usually head for home at a fast pace.

On large dogs it is best to use another measure. Fish and Wildlife Department trappers have a pole with a noose attached to release nontarget animals. The loose end of the rope runs down the pole through guides. The noose is fitted over the animal's muzzle and tightened so that it cannot open its mouth. While it is so held the trapper opens the trap, and when the leg is free, he loosens the tension on the noose so that the animal is able to pull free.

HOUSECATS

A housecat, feral or not, is a natural predator and a good one. It will take more than its share of small game such as quail, cottontail rabbits, grouse, and pheasants. If a cat is caught in a No. 2 trap or one smaller, the legbone will probably not be broken. A No. 3 or No. 4 will almost surely break the bone of the leg, and the animal should be humanely destroyed. Domestic cats will come to any trap set for a meat-eating animal. They are usually caught by one or both front legs.

The trapper should evaluate the catch as he did with the dog. If it is probable that the cat has gone wild, the trapper, unless he is a dyed-in-the-wool cat lover, should destroy it by giving it a good rap with the kill stick. If the trapper decides to release the animal, he should remember that, unlike the dog, the cat can scratch as well as bite. It is best to cover the animal completely with a coat or tarp. When the mouth and the claws are both immobilized the trap can be opened and the animal freed. The noose stick described for releasing dogs can also be used, but a cat, with its short muzzle, is difficult to noose over the jaws. Instead, slip the noose over the animal's head and tighten it around its throat. This will immobilize the animal, and in some instances, will cause it to become unconscious from lack of air. It can then be safely released.

BIRDS OF PREY

The best way to handle birds of prey is not to catch them in the first place. These hunters will seldom be caught in anything other than a bait set. They hunt by sight. If they cannot see the bait from the air they will not come to the set. Hide the bait so that it is not visible from the air and the trap will likely stay free of hawks, owls, eagles, ravens, crows, and vultures. However, even with a hidden bait, one will occasionally be caught. Maybe the predator lands near the set to capture a rodent and sees the bait nearby.

An eagle may see a fox, skunk, mink, or other small furbearer caught in a trap. Looking for a meal, it will come down, kill the animal, and devour part or all of it. Once the damaged or ruined animal has been removed by the trapper the eagle often returns to the site and gets caught even though no bait is used and the trap site is well cleaned up. Owls and large hawks may be taken in this same manner. They are seldom hurt seriously when caught, and they can easily be released. Although these birds will bluff

To release a hawk, take a wingtip with a gloved hand. The hawk will threaten with the beak, but the claws are the main offensive weapon. *(Photo: Gerry Blair)*

with their beaks, their primary weapon is their claws, and it is these the trapper has to look out for, not the beak. Most trapped birds will mantle their wings as the trapper approaches. This is a defensive stance to make them look bigger than they are. Take hold of one of the wing tips as the bird mantles and pull it to you so that the bird is held taut between the hand and the trap. Open the trap with the foot and pull the bird out of the trap. At the same time flip the bird away from you. It will stand on the ground mantling for a minute or two, and when it finally realizes that it is free will take off.

Treat an eagle with much more respect than other birds of prey. Put a kneeling cloth over the eagle to pin its free leg—this is the dangerous one. With a stick or large piece of cloth, grasp the free leg above the foot. Bring the foot over the trapped foot. Hold both legs together, open the trap, and carry the bird to an open area where it can fly. Toss it up and away from yourself. Eagles have such large feet that they are generally caught by a single toe and only their dignity has been hurt. Most of these hunters have very fast reflexes and will have almost pulled out before the trap closes, so they are not seriously hurt when released.

SMALL BIRDS

Any meat- or insect-eating bird will come to a baited trap. Jays are often caught if the trap tension is set too fine. To keep these nontarget critters from the trap, adjust the pan tension of the trap so that a bird will not be heavy enough to spring it. Many traps have a pan-tension adjustment built into the trap. For traps that do not have this adjustment feature, the trapper can cut a stick about the size of a kitchen match to fit under the pan. Cut a notch in the center of the twig so that it will break if the pan is depressed hard enough. This will increase the pan tension so that the trap will not spring from the weight of the bird. If the bird is caught in the trap, the trapper usually does not have to be concerned with release. The bird will almost always die in the trap, being caught high on the breast.

RODENTS AND RELATED ANIMALS

All manner of small animals will come to a baited trap, and some will come to lure or scent. The trapper can solve part of the problem by not using a cloth or canvas pan cover. More of the small animals can be kept from springing the trap by increasing the pan tension as described above. If the trap is in an area with a high population of squirrels, rabbits, or pack rats, you will have a constant problem keeping the animals from the trap and keeping the bait intact. Some trappers use rat traps baited with wet oatmeal to take out part of the overpopulation. There is no sure way, however, to keep these small critters away from the trap. If they get to be too much of a bother, you would be time ahead to move your set to a location which is not so popular with them.

ENDANGERED WILDLIFE

Infrequently, a trapper makes a catch of an animal that is threatened with extinction. Sometimes this animal has been placed on the endangered list and sometimes it has not. The black-footed ferret is an example of such a threatened animal. The kit fox and the ringtail cat also seem to be having a hard time. When these animals are caught, the trapper should make every effort to release them unharmed. All those mentioned are small animals and can be released either by using the noose stick or by covering them with a coat or tarp.

Some vocal anti-trappers have claimed loudly but falsely that

The ringtail cat will come to any set that will take a bobcat. They are uncommon in much of their range, and should be released if they are not badly hurt. *(Photo: Oregon Game Commission)*

dozens of nontarget animals are accidentally caught for each target animal caught. They have never supported their contention with facts, probably because they can't. If they do not trap themselves, they cannot know firsthand the target/nontarget ratio. Money trappers who depend on their traps for a living cannot afford to have them constantly filled with a nonpaying species, and they catch very few nonfurbearers.

In one twenty-month period between 1974 and 1976, a university student in northern Arizona did a study on the coyote to complete a master's thesis. He trapped coyote and released them

The black-footed ferret is rare to the point of extinction. If one shows up in a trap, release it and move the traps to another area. *(Photo: Duane Rubink, U.S. Fish and Wildlife Service)*

with radio collars to study their movements. He kept excellent records of the target and nontarget animals caught. His trapping produced fifty coyote catches, five bobcat catches, three striped skunk, one hognose skunk, one gray fox, and two badger. He was after coyote, so technically the other animals were nontarget, but all were furbearers and would be considered a target species by a trapper. He caught sixty-two furbearers. During the same period of time he caught six vultures, three rock squirrels, two porcupines, two cottontail rabbits, one jackrabbit, one raven, one horned owl, and one dog, for a total of seventeen nontarget animals. These nontarget catches for sixty-two target catches is not a bad average, particularly when one considers that the trapper was inexperienced. Proper precautions with hiding the bait could have eliminated the six turkey vultures, the horned owl, and the raven.

7
Trapping and the Law

Most of the states control the trapping of furbearers through a fish and game department. The regulations vary somewhat from state to state, but certain laws are almost universal. Some of the laws that govern trapping are designed to protect the furbearer in certain parts of its range and during certain parts of the year. Other laws are aimed to ensure that none of the species are overtrapped to the point that they will not reproduce and restock the area trapped. A few of the laws are laws of appeasement to anti-trappers.

PERMITS AND LICENSES
Most of the states that allow trapping require some form of registration with the state agency that controls trapping. The registration may be in the form of a free permit or may be a sold license. The states also usually require some sort of trap identification, either a number or initial stamped on each trap or a tied-on name tag. The license is issued to the individual named on the license only. Do not have your brother-in-law run the trapline for you when you get down with the flu. Most states will charge him with trapping without a license if he is caught, even if he is only running your line as a special favor. There is another danger in allowing someone else to run the line. The traps bear your name or identifier. Anything that goes wrong on the line will be your responsibility. Tend your own lines and avoid problems.

SEASONS
The trapping season varies from state to state, being largely determined by the time that the fur comes prime and stays prime. The average trapping season will open in early November and

close in late February. Many times, if the weather does not cooperate, the fur will be prime for only part of the season. The good trapper will not waste his time trapping fur that isn't prime. It is better to wait for cold weather and prime fur. The skins are just as much work to get before they are prime, and just as much work to care for. Better to let them reach their full price potential before taking them.

A fur may be prime and may still not bring the top dollar. The thickness and sheen of the outside fur is graded separately from primeness. Too, other factors may degrade a prime fur. Some animals rub the fur during the early spring months. Others go through a period when the hair singes or curls. Damage from mating activities will also decrease the value.

Different furbearers prime out at different times of the year. Coyote, bobcat, fox, skunk, mink, and marten will prime out in mid-November and will usually stay prime through January. By February the skunk, mink, and marten will begin to fade. By late February the coyote and the fox will begin to rub. March is the month when most muskrat reach prime, and they stay prime through April. So do the beaver. The exact prime periods will vary depending upon the part of the country and the current year's weather. Experience will teach the trapper the best times to trap to make the most from the fur.

TRAPPING NEAR ROADS

Many states have laws which make it illegal to trap within a certain distance of traveled roadways. The law helps to minimize complaints made to the fish and game departments about animals that are trapped and visible from the road. Even if there is no law against it in some states, the trapper would be well advised to stay away from roads. This generates a massive amount of bad publicity against all trappers, and the few animals that would be trapped are not worth the furor caused. The trapper should avoid the road trap for another very good reason. Trapped game that is visible from the road will not stay trapped for long. A passerby will soon steal the animal and the trap.

If you feel that you must place a set in a position that is visible from the road, and it is not against the law in your state, place the trap on a drag or a grapple so that the animal will be able to leave the area as soon as it is caught. It will be a simple matter to follow the drag trail to recover the animal. Usually, they will go to the nearest heavy brush where they can find a place to hide.

CAMPGROUNDS
Public campgrounds are also an area that the trapper would do well to avoid. Many states prohibit trapping here, and for a good reason. Many campers bring dogs and cats with them, and they should expect reasonable safety in such a place. Too, many of the campers have small children who might become caught in a trap and injured. There is plenty of other good trapping country available to the trapper.

RESIDENCES
Occupied homes are other areas that trappers should avoid. Again, many state laws are specific in spelling out the minimum distance that traps must be placed from houses. Common sense should prevail whether the law forbids it or not. No one would welcome a trap in his front yard. There would be an obvious danger to pets, livestock, poultry, and small children. Keep the traps in the remote areas of the land. There will be less anti-trapping sentiment, and the trapper will find that he gets along much better with his neighbors.

PRIVATE LAND
Most of the time, landowners will give permission to the trapper if they are approached in the right way. Most rural landowners have livestock and poultry which might be ready prey for the predatory species. Point out to the landowner that the trapping will decrease his losses to predators. Explain the precautions that you will take to prevent the capture of nontarget animals. Tell him how the traps will be placed to protect his livestock. If he is still not convinced and refuses permission, respect his right to manage his land as he sees fit. Thank him courteously and leave. Why make an enemy when you don't have to? The day may come when the landowner will contact you and make a request that you trap to assist him with a specific problem.

TRAPPER RESPONSIBILITY
The right to trap hangs by a single fragile thread in many parts of the country. The thread has already been broken in other areas,

and laws have been legislated which prohibit trapping of any kind. Whether the trapper is to be able to enjoy his profession and to profit from it in the coming years may be largely dependent on how responsibly he behaves. In addition to the comments listed previously in this chapter, he should conduct his activities in a way that will be least repugnant to nontrappers. Traps should be set so that they take the animal cleanly and minimize pain. Water or drown sets should be used when possible. The traps should be checked daily, and the run should be made as early in the day as possible. Animal carcasses should be discarded in a remote location so that they don't offend others.

The responsible trapper should concentrate his trapping efforts in areas where there is an overabundance of furbearers and avoid areas of minimal population. He should report to the proper law-enforcement agency any violations of the trapping or hunting code that he may witness. He should also tell the proper authorities of any diseased animals or wildlife that he encounters. He should willingly assist landowners who may have problems with predatory animals. He should make every effort to help train and encourage new trappers. It is to the advantage of all trappers that we be as good as we can be. A novice trapper, sometimes because of ignorance, may bring criticism to all trappers. We must share our knowledge and experience so that all trappers know the right from the wrong.

8
Trapping Geography

The type of country available to the trapper will dictate the direction of his trapping efforts. Each terrain has its own resident population of furbearers, and as the geography changes, so does the population density and the variety. If he is to be successful, the trapper must direct his main efforts at those furbearers that are most available to him.

TRAPPING THE DESERT

To many casual observers the low and high deserts of the West and Southwest are barren wastelands devoid of animal population. Although it is true that few animals are evident here during daylight hours, the desert comes alive at night with a startling array of animal numbers. Desert animals, for the most part, are night feeders. The high daytime temperature, particularly during the summer, drives most of them to underground burrows.

Most desert areas, the trapper will learn, support good populations of rabbits, ground squirrels, mice, and rats. When the rodents are present, the animals that prey on rodents will also be present. The bobcat, the coyote, and an occasional mountain lion are the large predators of the desert. Gray and kit fox are there too. So are the skunk—striped, spotted, and hognosed—the badger, the coati, and the ringtail.

To scout the area for trapping, inspect all of the dry washes that serve as runoff channels for the infrequent rains. The soft wash bottom is the highway of the desert, and each user will leave its mark in the soft sand. The dry wash is a good location for desert trapping. Choose a junction of two washes and put a scent-post set on the point of the junction. Most of the dog family, and many of

Left: This rock squirrel lives in the holes between big boulders. It would be a good location for a bobcat set.
Right: Coyotes like prairie dogs. Dog towns are good places to trap. *(Photos: Gerry Blair)*

the cats, will pause here in their travels to lift a leg and leave evidence of their passing. If the set is not made on the point of the wash, make it on the side of the wash that is closest to the prevailing wind. A set made there will let the wind carry the scent to all wash users and not away from them.

Many times, sand washes will be bordered with a narrow plateau of land. These tables are hotspots for rodents and will be the night hunting grounds of the predators. Use a bait set here and sweeten the pot with a bit of scent. This set, if properly made, will take bobcat, fox, skunk, badger, and once in a while coyote.

There are few real roads in the desert country. The trapper must run his line by foot, on horseback, or with a rough-country vehicle. Many Southwestern trappers work their lines with four-wheel-drive trucks. They run the sand washes with vehicles equipped with big tires that stay above the sand. The wash bottom

This coyote is hunting a line of brush in a gully. Rodents hide out in such areas. (Photo: Gerry Blair)

is not damaged by the travel; the first strong wind, or rain, will wash away all evidence of their passing. Other vehicle choices might be a trail-type motorcycle or a three-wheeled all-terrain vehicle.

Though water is scarce in the desert, there are a few major rivers that run year-round, some wet tributaries, and a scattering of man-made lakes and ponds. The available water attracts good numbers of rodents and rodent eaters. This is a good place to trap. In areas where water is scarce, much of the animal life has evolved into a community of nondrinkers—not even water. They get all of their nourishment from the plant material consumed, and in the case of meat eaters, from the liquid contained in their prey. The fact that there is no water present does not indicate a complete absence of furbearers.

The winter weather in the desert country is a joy to the

trapper. There is usually no snow and very little rain. The ground stays dry. Traps do not mud up or freeze up. The trapper can run his line wearing shirtsleeves most of the year. The fur, surprisingly, is long and prime. Well-handled fur from the desert will interest the buyer just as much as fur from the snow passes of the Rockies.

TRAPPING THE RIVER

Many of the furbearers depend on water and will not stray far into dry land. If the river is in the high mountain country and is mostly fast water, the trapper might expect to find mink, river otter, raccoon, fisher, marten, and beaver. Some of the large predators will also be present. Lynx, bobcat, mountain lion, and fox will be around in good numbers, and so will coyote. Check along the muddy banks of the streams to find tracks left in the mud. Look also for evidence of animal habitation. If there are beaver in the area, there will be gnawed trees and some points of the river or tributary will have lodges. Beaver dams will also be found.

Check the trails that cross the streams. Look particularly at the junction of two trails, or at the junction of a trail with a little-used road. You will see tracks in any soft area, and scat along trails and old roads.

TRAPPING THE LOW COUNTRY

In the lower country the rivers slow down and spread out. Often marshes and swamps are formed, creating good habitat for all water-loving furbearers. There will be beaver and probably muskrat. Raccoon, skunk, and weasel will be around. So will the mink. The larger carnivores will be present, usually in good numbers. While the main targets will be the water animals, the trapper can reap a bonus trapping coyote, bobcat, and fox.

Check the muddy banks for tracks. Walk the trails and look for tracks, scratches, and droppings. Beaver feed areas and beaver and muskrat lodges will be obvious. Spend an early morning or a late evening along the marsh and watch for beaver and muskrat swimming in the water. You can scout more country if you use a small boat to run the water's edge.

COLD-COUNTRY TRAPPING

Cold country has advantages and disadvantages over other ter-

Five wild horses slog across a swamp in western Arizona. Areas such as this produce beaver, muskrat, racoon, and other water-oriented fur bearers. *(Photo: E. E. Hertzog, Bureau of Reclamation)*

rain. When the snow is on the ground it is easy to scout for animal activity. Every critter that walks will leave a track in fresh snow. A good snow cover also permits the use of the snowmobile, which will go almost anywhere there is snow. A lot of ground can be covered in a short time. Animals that live in the cold country are always hungry, and they develop good long fur. They are fairly easy to trap because of their increased appetite. Caught animals are not likely to escape the trap. Many are quickly frozen and remain unspoiled in the trap until the trapper comes to collect.

Now for the bad news. Many times, in very cold country, the furbearers will migrate to lower country to spend the winter. Animal numbers may be down. The extreme low temperatures make it harder to make sets and keep them functional. If the days are warm enough to thaw the snow and then it refreezes at night, the traps will freeze up and will not spring. Sometimes the trapper cannot even find them until the spring thaw. And, of course, extreme low temperatures present some hazard for the trapper.

SELECTING A TRAPPING AREA

Every trapper dreams of a trapping area where there are huge numbers of furbearers and he has the sole trapping rights. Such areas are hard to find. Occasionally the trapper will locate a major landowner who will give him sole trapping rights, but most of the time the trapper will have to work public land in competition with a number of other trappers.

Pay a visit to the local office of the game department. The game managers usually issue the trapping licenses, and the local rangers should know which areas are heavily trapped. Conversations with the field men will often develop evidence of animal sightings or of sign left by desirable furbearers.

The local office of the government trapper might also be a fruitful place for information. These men are employees of the Animal Control Division of the U.S. Fish and Wildlife Service. As pointed out in Chapter 1, they trap to control damage, mostly predators; their trapping is usually done during the off season and they do not directly compete with the fur trapper. They do know, however, the range of most of the furbearers in the area and might be willing to share that information with an interested fur trapper.

9
Coyote

The coyote is a mammal with an average adult weight of 20 to 30 pounds. The weight varies between localities. In the northern mountain areas, as an example, coyote average heavier, perhaps as much as 40 pounds. Any coyote which weighs more than 50 pounds should be carefully checked. In some areas it could be a timber wolf, or more likely, a cross between a coyote and a dog.

The coyote is probably the smartest mammal with which man contends. It has a good nose, excellent eyesight, and a good brain with which it gathers and retains knowledge.

Color variation in the coyote fur is common. The coyote of the Pacific Coast is usually very dark. Coyote from Montana, Wyoming, and the Dakotas tend to be of a lighter variety. Many of the coyote of the Southwestern deserts tend to a red or roan color. There is also a wide color variation within the same habitat, and two coyote taken from the same set may exhibit a startling color variation.

Coyote are night hunters for the most part. Like other predators they time their hunting forays to when the prey species are out and about. If a coyote is hungry, however, it will hunt both day and night. Its favorite food is whatever is easiest to come by. If it has an empty belly it will eat and obtain nourishment from anything it can wrap a lip around. Near cities and populated areas the coyote will often visit garbage cans and piles. If it has the chance it will pick up a pet dog or cat while there. It will also raid the garden for watermelon, cantaloupe, ripe fruit, grain, and grasses. It will eat insects readily if they are available, most commonly grasshoppers. Near lakes and rivers the coyote will work the banks for dead fish. It is not much of a live fisherman, but will occasionally take one in shallow water. A coyote will eat any reptiles it can catch, including the poisonous varieties. The coyote has a built-in immunity to the venom and seldom dies from the occasional bite. In

The coyote is a night hunter most of the time. During the heat of the day it will hole up in a clump of brush. *(Photo: Gerry Blair)*

the Southwestern deserts the abundant reptile community is an important element in the coyote food chain. Birds will be taken, both adult and young, and so will the eggs if a nest can be located. Near lakes the coyote is an important predator of waterfowl. Large and small mammals, however, are the coyote's main diet. It will eat mice, rats, ground and tree squirrels, gophers, and rabbits. It will also take the young of most of the varieties of big game. Many wildlife biologists list the coyote as the most important predator of antelope and deer fawns. Coyote also take adult animals frequently. The adults are more easily killed during periods of deep snow when the coyote can move across the top of the crusted snow and the heavier prey sinks below the crust.

Most coyote mate during February—maybe earlier in the warmer states and a bit later in the north. Two months after breeding the pups are born. The litter averages four to six, and rarely is as high as twelve. The young are born in a den prepared by the female weeks before the pups are due. The den may be in a small natural cavern, a hole in a slide rock area, beneath abandoned buildings, under a large rock, or beneath the roots of a tree. The young are cared for by the mother. The male helps with the hunting and brings food for the hungry pups but is not allowed into the den. Sometimes a tolerated female, probably a pup from the last year's litter, assists the brood female in raising a large litter. As the young become able to travel they accompany the adults in the hunting forays. They are taught to hunt and to survive.

Only one breeding female is allowed to each territory. Thus, some female coyote may never breed. They must wait their turn to breed, either by finding and claiming a breeding territory of their own, or by inheriting a breeding territory from a breeder who dies. The trapping of a breeding female, then, may actually cause an increase in the coyote population. Her death may allow a younger female to claim a part of her territory and another female to claim another part. Two will be breeding in the same area instead of one.

The coyote family remains in contact in the home territory through the summer. They may separate within the territory on hunting forays, but keep in contact by yipping and howling. The howl system of the coyote is not totally understood, but it is certain that the howls communicate hunting patterns, territorial boundaries, family contact, and population and sexual advertisements. By early fall, the coyote pups are hunting by themselves. They still participate in the group hunts for rabbits and larger game, but are mostly off on their own.

Most adult coyote remain together as a pair until one dies. Within days the survivor finds and accepts a new mate. The new pair defends the territory with the same vigor as the old pair. Most other coyote respect the territorial boundaries of the pair, and those who do not are soon driven out. Some coyote are allowed into the territory as tolerated guests. These are probably the young from the previous year's litter. The tolerated coyote, however, are constantly reminded of their visitor status; they will be nipped above the hip area frequently by the landowners and will be forced to demonstrate their low station in life by lying on their backs with their feet in the air. If the population of the territory becomes a threat to the food supply, the tolerated coyote will be repeatedly attacked until they either leave or are killed.

The territorial boundaries of the coyote are established by howl points, scent posts, and coyote-to-coyote contacts. In late fall and winter, the tolerated coyote are usually forced to leave the home territory. This causes a continual movement of the young coyote as it searchs for its own home range. This movement can be

The trapper can sometimes get an estimate of coyote numbers in an area by spending a night there and listening for howls. (*Photo: Duane Rubink, U.S. Fish and Wildlife Service*)

used to good advantage by the trapper, as these young are traveling in country they do not know well and will usually stick to the trails and the sand washes. When the home-range coyote have been totally eliminated from an area, new coyote move in to claim the territory. This homesteading takes place within a few days, or at most a few weeks.

The home territory of a breeding female coyote varies somewhat depending upon the type of country and the availability of food. A study of radio-collared breeders in northern Arizona indicated a typical range of 8.1 square miles. The studies also established that the coyote moved within the total range seasonally—that is, the winter and summer ranges were separate portions of the total territory.

The coyote probably kills more game and domestic animals than all of the rest of the predators combined. This is due to its numbers and its nature. Sheepmen and cattlemen in the West know that the coyote is the main cause of calf and lamb losses. The coyote, and other predators, take a heavy toll on both big and small game; wildlife biologists estimate that more than 50 percent

of the young pheasants, quail, and grouse—all ground-nesters—
fall to predation.

VALUE AS A FURBEARER
Coyote fur, like the fur of other animals, fluctuates widely in price.
The price paid by the fur buyer will be governed by the fashion-
industry demands, the number of coyote pelts available, and the
size and condition of the hide. Coyote pelts in 1978 ranged from
$20 to $60, according to fur color and pelt condition. In Northern
states, at elevations between 6,000 and 10,000 feet, coyote pelts
are usually prime from mid-October until late January. In the
Southern, warmer, states, and at lower altitudes, the fur may not
prime out until late November. Hair singe or curl, caused by lying
in the sun, may start in January and is usually evident in all pelts
taken after mid-February. Hip rubbing and shedding may begin in
February. The rubbing and shedding will depend, of course, on
the current year's weather. Trappers earn the best price from
prime coyote that have been properly skinned, stretched,
cleaned, and stored.

COYOTE TRAPS
There are a number of methods available for taking coyote. The
snare has been used with limited success. Deadfalls will also take
coyote, but not in great numbers. Poisons such as strychnine and
10-80 have been successfully used in predator-control programs,
but have little to offer the fur trapper who wants the animal to
remain alive until he can visit the trap and collect it. The predator
call, which imitates the sound of an injured rabbit, will also lure a
fair number of coyote within rifle range. Many trappers use the
call while on the trapline and pick up an extra number of coyote
every year. The main tool of the trapper, however, is the trap. The
modern steel trap is an efficient fur getter. It is light in weight,
easily hid, does not unduly damage the animal, and is humane if it
is used properly.

TRAPS FOR COYOTE
Coyote have been trapped and held in traps that were really much
too small for coyote trapping, and they have escaped from traps
that were the right size. Generally, the best trap for the coyote is a
No. 3 double-spring, a No. 3 coil-spring, or a No. 3 jump trap. The
coil spring and the jump trap are lighter than the double-spring.

The No. 3 double-spring trap works well for coyote. If caught correctly, by a front foot and above the pad, the coyote will not pull out. *(Photo: Bill Musgrove)*

and they are easier to hide. Any of the traps manufactured at the present time will take coyote if they are the right size and if they are properly used. The brand name of the trap is best left to the personal preference of the trapper.

A coyote trap is secured in three general ways: by tying down to a solid object, by tying to a drag or a grapple, or by tying down to a stake driven into the ground. The solid tiedown and stake is used by most trappers. This holds the animal at the set site. The catch does not have to be tracked down or hunted to be retrieved. Traps must be set so that the foot is well caught. The drag or the grapple will often prove to be the best choice. The trapped animal will be able to pull a short distance away from the set and will usually head for the nearest brushy area to hide. It can be trailed by the marks left by the drag.

READING COYOTE SIGN

The area to be trapped should be scouted, preferably well before the actual trapping season begins. Early fall is a good time to

Droppings will tell the trapper where the animal feeds. These coyote droppings show that the animal has been feeding on prickly pear. *(Photo: Gerry Blair)*

scout, as the coyote will have moved into the winter range by then. Spend a night in the area if possible and listen for the howl patterns. Many times the howls will pinpoint concentrations, general territories, and hunting areas. Coyote will leave tracks, scratchings, droppings, and evidence of feeding to advertise their presence. Certain areas of the territory will be apt to hold a record of coyote movement.

Droppings

Coyote droppings are about the size and shape of the droppings left by a medium-sized dog. The appearance of the feces varies. If the coyote is eating mostly meat or carrion the droppings will appear black and will usually have a large amount of hair visible. If the coyote has been eating the fruit of the prickly pear cactus, the scat will be red with the peelings from the pears and will contain seed. If times are hard and the coyote is existing on the stingy berry of the juniper tree, the droppings will have a pink cast and contain numerous seeds. Deer, rabbit, antelope, and small rodents all leave distinctive evidence in the offal. The good trapper, by knowing what the animal is eating, will know where he is most likely to be found.

Scratches

A coyote leaves urine at predictable points within its territory. The urine marks the territorial boundaries, and those boundaries will often coincide with major geological features, such as a large canyon, a point of a ridge, or the perimeters of a mesa. Scent is also left at waterholes, at the point where two trails intersect, points where trails cross old roads, and at the corner post of a fence that parallels a trail. Both droppings and scent are left at the carcass of a decaying animal such as a cow, deer, elk, or antelope. Even when the meat has been eaten and the remains consist of bone, hair, and stink, the coyote will come back at regular intervals, either to hunt one more bite of food or to roll in the rotting remains. A good trapper notes these locations as sites for future sets.

Tracks

A coyote track is like the track of a medium-sized dog, only it is usually smaller. It will be found in the soft dirt of a game trail or a cattle trail. Sand washes and the muddy banks of streams and lakes also show tracks. In snow, every coyote who passes through will leave its mark. A fresh snow is an excellent time to go afield and inspect the trapping territory. The trapper will learn coyote numbers, distribution, and hunting paths, and can make a rough map of the coyote movement in the area. The memory is faulty and too much information will be lost if it is not put on paper.

There is little chance that a coyote track will be mistaken for a fox track or a cat track. The fox track is much smaller, and most of the time will show a double imprint where the hind foot comes to rest in the same track that the front foot made. The bobcat or the lynx will make a bigger track than the coyote, and the track will be more round with a different-shaped heel pad.

Play Area

The coyote will often have a "playground" area where coyote from adjoining territories will come to run, slide, jump, and dig. The area will usually be a flat that contains low brush and a quantity of loose dirt or sand. The players are mostly the coyote of the current year. Older coyote will watch the frolic and will occasionally join in to show the youngsters who is boss. Many times the play will be accompanied by much yipping and howling. The play area will be used on a continuing basis, and two dozen coyotes may be taken from such an area during the course of a season.

HELP FROM THE RANCHER

The rancher who works the trapping area can be a good friend to the trapper. It will pay to visit the rancher before the season and obtain his permission to trap. In certain parts of the West the rancher only leases his grazing rights from the state or federal government and has no real claim to the game, but even in those instances it is best to get permission. Most ranchers are not a friend of the coyote and will readily agree to the trapping operation. Visit the rancher from time to time during the season to show him the coyote you have trapped. He will usually be cooperative and will often tell you the locations of coyote concentrations, freshly dead stock, and other information that will be helpful. Both of the authors make it a point to visit the rancher at season's end to discuss the catch and thank him for his hospitality. If the catch has been good, a small present might be in order, perhaps a fifth of his favorite beverage. These small courtesies help to ensure your welcome for the coming season.

SETS FOR COYOTE

There are four basic sets used by the successful coyote trapper. Each one of these sets has a number of variations. They are discussed below in their relative order of importance.

Scent-Post Set

All coyote deposit scent at predetermined points within their territory. Like other members of the dog family they have a compulsion to leave scent at any point where another coyote has urinated. These are excellent sites for trap sets. If a natural scent-post area cannot be located, it is a simple matter to make one. If it is located in an area where coyote are apt to pass it will take them as readily as a natural post.

To make a scent-post set, find a small bush or a dead stick that is located near a trail, at the point where two washes come together, the point of two canyons, or the corner post of a fence. Use the kneeling tarp to prevent your knees from touching the ground and leaving human scent, and dig two holes large enough to

A rotting animal carcass, or part of a carcass, is a good area for a scent-post set. Dig a hole large enough to hide the drag, stake, and trap. Put the hole slightly to the left or right of the nose. Use the kneeling tarp and rubber gloves.

If a stake is used, drive the stake into the hole so that the trap will be bedded on top of the stake.

If a drag or a grapple is used, bury it under the trap or slightly to the side. Wax the chain and grapple in the same manner as the traps.

accommodate the traps. Put the free jaw of the trap back against the bush edge. Place the traps about one coyote step apart. Most areas have a prevailing wind direction, and the trapper should always choose his set site so that the prevailing wind blows from the traps to the trail. The holes should be just large enough to

Position the trap and fill in the springs with dirt. Bed the free jaw with packed dirt or a small rock. Put pan cover in place and weight down with a small amount of dirt.

Use a small stick or wire to tuck the pan cover under the jaws of the trap.

Use the dirt sifter to completely cover the trap. Use a stick or small broom to level the ground. Make the set appear natural by sprinkling pine needles or leaves over the fresh dirt.

Spray coyote urine on the nose area of the head. Note natural appearance of the set. Back away from the set and use a branch to smooth away your tracks. *(Photos: Gerry Blair)*

accept the traps. Put the dirt from the digging on the front of the kneeling cloth. Drive the trap stake, if one is used, into the ground at the bottom of the dug-out hole. If a drag or grapple is used, bury that at the bottom of the hole. Position the trap above the stake or drag. Rubber gloves must be worn to keep the human scent from the traps and the stake. Put the pan cover over the set trap. If the wind is blowing, hold the pan cover in position with one hand and sift a small amount of dirt on it. This will hold the pan cover in position until it can be adjusted properly. Then use a small stick, about the size of a pencil, to tuck the edges of the pan cover under the inside edge of the trap jaws. The pan cover, of course, will have been slit on the side where the trap dog fits. Sift more dirt over the trap, covering the springs first if it is a long spring trap, and then the area covered by the pan cover. Keep adding dirt until the trap depressions are brought up to the level of the surrounding ground. Use the dirt from the kneeling tarp that was saved from the digging of the hole. When the desired level has been reached, use a stick or a brush to level the dirt above the traps so that they look completely natural. Remove the remaining dirt from the kneeling tarp by carrying it away from the set and scattering it downwind.

The set has now been prepared to take the smartest coyote. All that is needed is the addition of scent. Take a small stick about ¼ inch in diameter and 6 to 8 inches long and dip it in the scent or lure. Place the stick on the bush several inches above the ground and midway between the two traps. Spray urine from the urine bottle on the bush just above the scent stick. The lure will call the coyote to the set, and the urine will encourage him to urinate. If the traps have been properly placed he will place a foot, or in some cases two feet, in one or both.

If the trap is set during the rainy season, place a small flat rock or a cow chip at an angle over the stick that holds the scent. This will serve as a roof to prevent the rain from washing away the lure before it has a chance to do its job.

If the set is made in subzero weather, instead of using dirt to cover the trap use pulverized cow manure. It is less apt to freeze.

If the set is made with a single trap, place the scent or lure 8 inches in from the jaws of the trap. Two traps to a set is much preferred. It will double the chance of a catch and will sometimes make a double leg catch. The main trap of a set is placed to make a front-foot catch. A coyote caught by a front foot does not twist off easily. A front-foot catch also prevents the animal from lunging against the tiedown and possibly pulling it out. Too, a front-foot catch does not allow the coyote to travel as far away from the set if a drag or a grapple is used.

When the set is as perfect as it can be, gather all your equipment and step to the back edge of the kneeling tarp. Use a long green limb to smooth the area you knelt upon to set the trap. Gather the tarp and the remaining dirt and back away from the set. Throw the dirt far enough away from the set to keep from alarming the customers.

The Dirt-Hole Set

A dirt-hole set can be used to good effect in any type of terrain. The hole used may be a badger hole, the hole left by a predator digging out a rodent, or a hole you make yourself. The actual size of the hole does not seem to matter. The principle of the set is basic. The hole is baited with a fish-oil or chunk bait and partially covered with dirt. The trap or traps are set in the loose soil at the mouth of the hole. The coyote assumes that another predator has had a meal here and has left part of it for an early return. In digging out the cache the coyote is caught by a front foot.

If you dig your own hole, put it at the foot of a low bank, a rock, or a low bush. Do not use anything for a backing that the coyote cannot see over. It is aware that it is stealing another predator's food and will want to keep a sharp eye for the return of the owner. The backing will force the coyote to approach the set from the correct position to spring the trap. Dig straight into the bank if that is the backing selected. If the hole is on level ground it should be dug at a 45-degree angle. The bait should be far enough into the hole so that the coyote cannot reach it without digging. Place the trap 8 inches back from the lip of the hole and 2 or 3 inches to the right of center. If two traps are used, place them 4 to 6 inches back from the lip of the hole, one 6 inches to the left of center and the other 6 inches to the right of center.

With larger dirt holes, use the loose dirt at the mouth of the hole to cover the traps. A drag or a grapple should be used to permit the trapped animal to leave the area without undue damage to the set. As in the scent-post set, the drag or grapple should be buried in the dirt beneath the trap.

Fresh bait, such as a rabbit, or prepared and rotted chunk bait

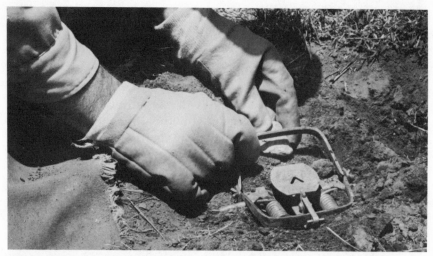

Above: To make a dirt-hole set, dig a hole 8 inches deep and 4 inches across. If one trap is used, place it back from the hole about 6 inches and slightly to the right of center. Place a small rock under the free jaw to anchor it.

Below: If two traps are used, place the second trap in line with the number-one trap and slightly to the left of center. *(Photos: Gerry Blair)*

can be used. A small stick with lure can also be placed in position at the top lip of the hole but should not be used on all dirt-hole sets. A trapwise coyote will soon associate the lure with the trap and will avoid every set where the lure is present. With sets of both types, the trapper increases his chances of catching the smart old ridge runner. Rotten chunk bait works best in areas of high rodent population, as they are less apt to bother the bait if it is rotten.

The traps are covered with pan covers and dirt in the same manner used for the scent-post set. Again, use the kneeling tarp and rubber gloves. Finish off with a tree branch, brushing out all evidence of your presence.

The Blind Set

A blind set is a set made without the use of lure, scent, or bait. The trap is concealed in a place that the coyote is likely to visit. Sticks, rocks, or bits of cactus are sometimes used to encourage the coyote to put its foot in the trap. A dim trail leading to a rotting carcass might be a good spot for a blind set. So would a point under a fence that shows evidence of coyote crossings. Look for bits of hair caught in the barbs of the fence as the coyote crawls under. The blind set can be made at the point of a rock or at the end of a high bank. When making a blind set, check the trail for tracks of cattle or wild animals. Deer and cattle will step into a blind set as readily as a coyote, and while they usually pull loose with little trouble, the set is ruined and the trap may be damaged. A step-over stick or rock can be placed in the trail so that the coyote will not miss the trap. The traps of a blind set should be placed so that the trap jaws are parallel with the travel of the coyote. The trap pan should be about 5 inches away from the step-over stick. The trap should be attached to a drag so that the caught animal will leave the area with minimal damage to the trap site.

The digging, covering, finishing, and tiedown of the traps in the blind set will follow the same procedure used in the construction of the scent-post set. If a drag is used, and it should be, a homemade lead drag weighing about 15 pounds can be buried under the trap. A rock can also be used, with a wire harness wrapped around the rock and the trap chain wired to the harness. A good-sized limb of a tree can also be used as a drag. All that is needed is an object which will prevent the coyote from going far and will leave a trail for the trapper to follow.

The Bait Set

Bait sets using dead rabbits or dead livestock are effective. Many states, however, have laws that prohibit the placing of a trap within a certain distance of a bait. If the bait set is legal in your state, tie down the bait at the edge of a bush or slightly under the bush. Set one or two traps about 10 inches back from the bait. Cover and finish off as in the scent-post set.

If the traps are to be set at the carcass of a dead livestock animal, a different procedure should be followed. If the carcass is freshly dead, do not set traps until the coyote have started feeding on it. Put two traps 8 inches out from the head and two traps 8 inches out from the area which shows the most feeding activity. If you have extra traps, put two out 8 inches from the hip area. All of the traps should be on drags, as the coyote will frighten off new customers if it is chained to the spot. With a drag it is able to leave and the trapper has a good chance of making another catch at the carcass. The authors have taken three coyote in one night, and ten coyote from one carcass, using this system. The procedure for trap setting is the same as for the scent-post set. Dig the hole, bury the drag, set and place the trap, position the pan cover, and finish off the set to look natural. Use rubber gloves, of course, and the kneeling tarp. You may want to squirt a couple of streams of urine at the head of the carcass.

If the law prohibits the setting of traps adjacent to the carcass, move off the required distance and make a number of scent-post and lure sets. Blind sets will also work here.

Old dried-up carcasses of large wildlife and livestock also attract coyote. They are natural scenting areas and smelling locations. If the entire dried-up carcass is still intact, make two sets. Two traps at the head and two at the hips seem to produce the best results. Both of the trap sets should be tied to weighted grapples. Use coyote urine and gland scent on the head of the carcass and place the traps 2 or 3 inches away from the head. Use a small piece of chunk bait at the hip set. The bait can be stuck to the bones or the hide. Conceal the traps 8 to 10 inches away from the carcass. An old carcass can be used by the trapper for many years. The coyote get into the habit of visiting the spot and there is a lot of coyote scent around. Too, many times coyote will roll in the carcass, as they seem to enjoy the smell of rotting flesh.

Coyotes will often patrol fence lines hoping to discover prey animals there. These are good areas for scent-post sets. *(Photo: Duane Rubink, U.S. Fish and Wildlife Service)*

LOCATIONS FOR SETS

One basic set can be used effectively in various special locations, sometimes with slight variations.

Sand-Wash Sets

Sand-wash sets are always coyote getters because the coyote uses the sand wash as a highway. A trapper should check the sand of the wash to find which part of the wash the coyote normally travel. A scent-post set or a lure set and a dirt-hole set will take every coyote that comes along if set correctly. If stakes are used, be sure to have extra-long stakes attached also to drags. The soft sand does not hold a stake well, and the drag is insurance in case the trapped animal pulls the stake. Lone small bushes, points of rock, or the sharp point of a bank are all good bets. When trapping sand washes, particularly in a vehicle, keep an eye on the weather. A dry wash can turn into a raging torrent in short order, and the unwary trapper may lose his traps, his vehicle, and his life.

Water Sets

Although the coyote is a land animal it can often be taken in a water set. Fasten a bait to a stake and put the stake 2 or 3 feet from the bank. The water should be about 3 to 6 inches deep. Place two or three traps attached to drags between the bait and the bank. The coyote will walk shallow water readily without paying attention to what is between it and the bait. No trap-pan cover or dirt cover, of course, is needed in this set. Small running streams, lake banks, and the edges of dirt-tank waterholes are all good bets for the water set. A trapper can make the sets by walking in the water with hip or knee boots, or by working from a small boat. Either system leaves no scent.

Fence Sets

Around farming or ranching areas, or anywhere one finds a fence, are good places to make a coyote set. A hole in a woven wire fence and a crawl hole under a woven wire fence are natural areas for a blind set. Set the traps about a foot back from the fence and put them on the side that does not contain livestock. If there are no livestock on either side put one trap on each side of the fence. Tie down to a weighted grapple or other drag to allow the animal to leave the set. Otherwise it will damage the set and make it difficult to catch a second coyote at the same spot.

Snow Sets

Snow or frozen ground makes the job of the trapper more difficult. With the right technique, however, sets can be made that will take fur. Heavy wax paper should be used as the pan cover, as canvas pan covers hold the moisture and will freeze up at night. When frozen they are as stiff as a board and would not spring if John Wayne stepped on them. The wax will not freeze. If the set is to be placed in a timbered area, make the set under the branches of a tree. Usually a ground mass of needles or leaves has built up over the years. This will make it easier to dig if the ground is frozen. Use dry dirt, dry leaf parts, or dry cow manure for the material above the trap. Pick the south side of the tree, as the extra sun will help keep the set dry. Shredded juniper needles make a good trap covering. The longer needles of the pine family are not as good; they will often clog the trap and allow the animal to escape. Fresh loose snow can sometimes be used as a trap cover. If the snow is drifting, however, or if the weather melts the snow during the day and freezes it at night, this set is not worth the effort.

The anthill set can often be used with good results when there is snow on the ground. The loose sand, leaves, grass, and other debris of the hill can be used to hide the trap. Being above ground level, or snow level, the trap is less likely to freeze up. The material of the hill is usually very dry and makes a trap-covering material that is not apt to freeze.

Rainy weather causes many coyote trappers to pull their sets and head for home, but the rain can be used as an ally that will help the trapper to take more fur. The rain washes human odor away from the trap site and makes the coyote more confident. Use larger stakes when setting traps in muddy ground, as the holding power of the ground is reduced. Bed the trap with leafy material or pulverized manure. Place the wax-paper pan cover in position and finish off the trap with sifted manure or sand over the trap. The underspring jump trap seems to do the best job in a wet-weather set. Any scent or lure placed in the open will be promptly removed by the rain, so place the scent or lure under a tilted cow chip or under a flat rock about hand size. A sand wash with pure sand is a good place for the wet-weather set, because the sand is not as apt to mud up as other sets. Many times a wet-weather set in a sand wash needs no other bedding material. Rainy weather will put the coyote on the move and it will cover more ground than it would otherwise.

SNARES

Snares have been used to take coyote for many years, and while they are not generally as effective as steel traps, they can sometimes be used to take an educated coyote that cannot be caught in a steel trap. When snared, the coyote kills itself soon after it is caught and is not likely to escape. Snares have other advantages. They are light and can be carried long distances on a trapline, they cost less than steel traps, and they are inconspicuous when set and are less apt to be stolen.

Snares also have certain disadvantages. They will sometimes take nontarget animals such as dogs and cats, and these animals are also killed. The nontarget animals taken in a leghold trap, of course, can be released, usually unharmed. Snares are not as versatile.

Snares must be cleaned and waxed the same as steel traps. Snare sets should be made along trails, at crawl holes under fences, at log crossings, and at prepared bait sets. When a snare is used along a trail that is used by big game and livestock, lean a pole across the trail with one end on the ground and the other end raised slightly above the ground. Leave enough room under the raised end to let the coyote walk through. This will keep larger animals away from the snare. Small trails through thick brush are good bets for snare sets. The loop of the snare should be about 10 inches in diameter and the bottom of the loop should be 10 inches above the ground. A small stick can be positioned between the bottom of the loop and the ground to force the coyote to lift its head and not go under the snare. Use small wire or small branches to keep the snare loop in the correct position. The snare can be tied off to a tree, a rock, or a drag. In some Northern states, snares are whitewashed rather than waxed to get a better blend with the snow. The No. 2 Kleflock snare with or without the swivel works well on coyote. The swivel will tend to keep the snare from kinking, however, and the swiveled snare will have a longer useful life.

CHECKING THE LINE

Most state law requires the trapline to be checked daily. Make it a habit to start out early and check the traps as soon after daylight as possible. Most predators are caught at night, and if they are removed from the trap early they will fight the trap less and will therefore be less likely to escape. An early check also helps to combat trap thieves.

Do not walk any nearer the coyote trap than is absolutely necessary. Every visit will leave some scent of human presence. If you're using a vehicle, either truck, snowmobile, or motorcycle, do not leave the vehicle to check the trap if you can avoid it. Some sets can be checked with binoculars. Many old-time trappers would place a small leafy limb from a tree into the ground and run it through one of the trap-chain links. When an animal was caught it would pull the branch down and the trapper could tell the set was sprung from a long distance.

There will be times when the set has not been sprung but will need adjustment. The wind sometimes removes the top dirt and exposes a part of the trap or the pan cover. If you must approach the trap to make an adjustment—to collect a furbearer, or to release a nontarget animal—proceed as you did when the trap set was originally made. Use rubber gloves, use the kneeling tarp, and brush out your tracks and scent with the leafy part of a tree limb. Some trappers work at a full-time job and run their lines before or after work. Sometimes the run is made in the dark. Use a good hand-held spotlight to check the traps from the vehicle. The less often you walk around the trap set, the more coyote you will take.

REMOVING TRAPPED COYOTE
When a coyote is caught in a trap, you should evaluate the catch from a distance, because if the animal is barely caught in the trap it will likely pull out if you approach too close. It is best to shoot these toe catches rather than risk losing them.

When walking up to a trapped coyote, consider every one dangerous. The bite can be severe, and too, there is always the danger of rabies. Most trappers use a kill stick to put the animal away. Hit the trapped animal just forward of the eyes with the stick. While it is unconscious, use your knee or the heel of your shoe to come down hard behind the front leg. This ruptures the heart, and the coyote never regains consciousness. This is a fast and humane way to deal with the animal. The chest cavity fills with blood and there is no external bleeding to stain the fur. If the animal is shot there is usually some blood that gets on the fur and on the ground, and any blood that hits the ground must be removed if the trapper hopes to catch another coyote at the set.

To make sure a coyote is dead, take a small stick and touch one of the eyeballs lightly. If the animal is completely dead there will be no blink reflex in the eye. Remove the dead coyote from the trap and lay it aside out of the way. Check the trap stake or tiedown for looseness. Check all wire connections for sign of kinking or stress. With rubber gloves on, rub sand or coarse dirt around the jaws of the trap to remove the blood if there is any present. Do not remove any urine the coyote passed while he was in the trap, because this will make the set more attractive to the next coyote that comes by. If the coyote has scratched and dug up a circular area around the set, move the traps to the side of the circle. Put them where the prevailing wind will blow from the traps to the trail. A coyote that comes to the area will walk around the circle and explore the new set location if you have made a scent set.

If the coyote has been caught in a set with a drag or a grapple, follow the trail left by the drag until you find the coyote. Kill the animal and remove it from the trap. Use rubber gloves to handle the trap and drag, and return it to the set. If you are following a coyote pulling a drag or a grapple at night, remember that the animal has about 6 feet of loose chain between it and the weight. That is a lot of distance to work with if it decides to lunge. It is better to take no chances at night. Shoot the animal.

Do not drag the coyote on the ground when taking it to the vehicle. This will damage the fur and reduce the value of the pelt. It will also get the pelt dirty and make extra work. Place the coyote in the vehicle where it will not get dirty. Many open-bed pickups throw mud in wet weather, and if the coyote is not protected it will likely be a ball of mud by the time you finish your rounds.

SKINNING

Coyote should be skinned within a few hours after they are killed. If the weather is warm the inside of the belly will soon turn green from the action of the strong stomach acids, and this will reduce the value of the pelt. If the coyote needs washing, either because of mud or blood, it can be done either before or after skinning. The fur dries more quickly if the washing is done before skinning. If the coyote pelt is likely to get bloody during skinning it is best to wash after skinning.

To skin a coyote, use a sharp pocket knife and split the inside of the hind legs from the under-foot side to just forward of the anal opening. Cut around the anal opening. Make a ring around the leg just above the pad on each hind foot. Pull the hide away from the body. If the hide does not come free with moderate pressure, use the knife to cut the inside of the hide away from the meat. Also use the knife to work the tail skin away from the tail. You will be able to work it loose for about 3 or 4 inches away from the rump, when it will bind and come no further. Use two small sticks about pencil size to hold each side of the skinned part of the tail. Grab the base of the tail in a firm grip and pull up on the tail and at the same time pull the two sticks down against the fur. The bone should pull completely from the tail fur.

Fasten the coyote by a rope tied to a hind foot so that the head is several feet above the floor. Pull and cut the hide loose until the front legs are reached. Pull the front legs up and out of the hide and skin them out. Cut the hide free of the front legs by cutting a ring around the leg just above the first joint above the foot. If the foot is bloody from trap injury, cut the hide above the injury and then cut the leg completely off just above the injured area. This will prevent the hide from getting bloody as it is pulled over the foot. Pull the hide on down to the ears, cutting with the knife as needed. The ears can be felt as lumps under the hide. Cut the ear cartilage loose from the head and continue skinning out the head. Cut the eyes loose from the head by using the knife close to the skull. The black rims around the eyeball should come off with the hide. Skin on down to the nose and cut the tip of the nose loose from the head. Again, the black tip of the nose stays together with the hide.

If the nose of the coyote is bleeding because of injury from the killing stick or from being shot, tie a plastic bag over the head before skinning. This will prevent nose blood from contaminating the fur as it is pulled over the head. Put paper towels in the bag to soak up any blood that falls in the bag. When the coyote is skinned down to the head area, untie it from the hanger and take off the plastic bag. Wipe the head clean of blood with more paper towels and then tie the coyote back up, only this time, tie it with its head in the air and the hind feet hanging down. Tie the coyote by pulling the fur up over the head and tie off to the fur that has already been loosened. The coyote's weight will pull down against the fur and make it easier to skin out the head. Too, in this position, the wound in the coyote's head will not bleed, as gravity forces the blood back down into the chest cavity.

When the skin is removed from the carcass, take it to the fleshing board to remove any meat or fat left by the skinning. All burrs or matted hair should be removed from the fur before fleshing. Otherwise the fleshing knife is apt to cut the hide at the point where it is raised. A solid board should be used for the fleshing. There are many fleshing tools on the market, and most of them do a good job, though an old putty knife will do it about as well.

Remove all of the fat from the hide, but do not cut too close to the skin. No hair should come off with the scraper. When the fat and the remaining flesh have been taken off, cut the tail from the base to the tip by making one long slit. This will let the air in and help to dry out the inside of the tail, reducing the danger of the inside of the tail spoiling and causing the tail hair to slip.

Wipe the inside of the hide with paper towels to remove any free fat or oil left from the fleshing. Use the pocket knife to cut away excess fat and flesh from the ear and mouth areas.

The pelt is now ready to be stretched out. It should be as long as the pelt will allow. Put the hide on the stretching boards (see Chapter 4) with the fur side in and the flesh side out. Pull the pelt onto the boards and tack the nose in place. Pull the hide as far down on the stretcher as it will come and tack the bottom in place. Now pull the bottom ends of the boards as wide as the hide will allow and nail them into place. The pelt should be about 12 inches wide at the hips. Finish tacking the jaw area.

To dry the pelt, find a place that is out of the sun, is dry, and has a good air circulation. Watch the hide until it is almost dry. The time varies depending upon the weather conditions. When the hide is almost dry, it is ready for turning. Remove the tacks or nails that hold it to the board and remove from the stretching board. The crosspiece that holds the boards taut will have to be removed to get the hide off. When the hide is off the board, turn the front legs first. Use a pair of longnose pliers to reach inside the front legs and grab hold of the ends and pull them through. Turn the head next by pushing it down inside the skin cavity. Keep working until the head and shoulders are pushed down where they can be reached by running the hand up the inside of the pelt, and grab hold of the nose and pull the skin on through. The fur should be fur side out now and is ready to go back on the stretcher. Tack it back into position and leave it until it is completely dry. Remove it from the stretcher and hang it up in a cool dry place with good air circulation until it is ready to be sold.

Sometimes the hide will become too dry, particularly around the front legs and shoulders, to turn properly. If that happens, use a moistened paper towel or rag to wet the areas that are too dry. Keep working these areas until they loosen up and the hide can be turned.

SPECIAL PROBLEMS

All trappers will encounter special problems in coyote trapping that will cause their hair to turn gray early. A trapper who has no problems in dealing with the coyote doesn't do much trapping. Those special problems that the authors have encountered are listed now, with suggestions for remedies.

Livestock

Cattle and burros seem to be attracted to a bait-hole set about as readily as the coyote. They will trample the set and spring the traps. The trapper, of course, will catch no fur while the traps are sprung, and he will have to rebuild the set. These animals seem to be brought to the set by the chunk bait. If cattle start bothering the sets, back off on the chunk bait and use more gland scents and urine. Set the trap a bit closer to the bush or the lip of the hole, to help keep these large animals' feet away from the trap.

Deer

Deer will come to any kind of bait and lure, and to many of the gland scents. If deer are springing the traps, use a mixture of coyote urine and skunk scent on the trap set. A coyote-gland scent is also good. Even these, however, will call some deer. If the trapper is using No. 3 or smaller traps, the deer will pull out of the trap quickly with no injury. Anything larger will probably hold the deer and it will injure itself as it struggles for release.

Tracks Around the Set

When a coyote comes to a set, looks it over, and turns and runs, it is a smart coyote. It has seen or smelled something wrong about the set. It may have lost a toe at a set using a similar scent or lure. Dirty traps with the smell of oil or human scent will also warn it off. You may want to pull the traps and replace them with clean fresh ones. Change the type of scent or lure used on the set. Check the set carefully for any steel or pan cover that may have been uncovered by the wind. Brush out any tracks you may have left at the set. Check also for tracks that may have been left by another individual at the set. The coyote will probably return for another look at the set, and if the defect has been corrected it may well be caught.

At times a coyote will dig out the traps and not be caught. This signals an odor on the traps, either human or oil, and the coyote's nose tells it where they are hidden. Sometimes this is a sign of poorly bedded traps or traps covered with a soil not found at the trap site. Make a fresh set nearby using new traps and attempting to correct the defect that warned off the coyote.

Rodents

The use of cloth pan covers is the biggest reason that rodents come to a trap. They will dig around the traps and either uncover them or spring them. Changing to the wax paper pan cover will often cure the problem. Rodents sometimes dig into the trap because they sense a cavity beneath the trap pan. It is their nature to explore such cavities, and they will spoil a set. Any unusual odor of the waxed traps will also attract digging. If the trap is covered with fine dust or sand, the rodents will often take a dust bath and spring the trap. If this is the case, try using a coarser grit of sand. If rodents persist, some can be taken out of the trap area by setting large rat traps baited with moistened oatmeal.

Other Nontarget Animals

Hawks, eagles, and ravens all come to a trap that is baited. So do ground squirrels, rabbits, and small birds. Most of the small game can be kept out of the trap by adjusting the pan tension so that these lightweights can't spring the pan. On traps that do not have an adjustment, cut a small stick about the size of a kitchen match to put under the pan. If the stick is between the pan and the trap frame, it will increase the weight needed to spring the trap and will not catch these small freeloaders. The V opening of the Victor trap can be used to insert the small stick at an angle between the pan and trap frame. Other traps must have an ⅛-inch or ¼-inch hole drilled in the pan. Do not use a matchstick. The odor of sulfur on the wood might warn off a smart coyote. Using a stick the size of a pencil under the pan and over the upper spring rings between the jaws is a method used by many old-timers in the trapline. Make sure the ends of the stick will not be caught by the closing jaws. Wool, foam rubber, or cotton may be used under the pan of the trap to produce more tension. These materials will absorb water, however, and will freeze up the trap in cold weather.

To keep large birds of prey from the traps, do not use a bait that is visible from the air. These birds find their dinner by using their eyes. If they cannot see the bait from the air they probably will not come to the trap.

MOVING THE LINE

A good trapper usually moves his line about every two weeks. If he knows his business he will have taken most of the coyote, fox, and cat from an area in that length of time. The animals left will be the old smart ones that will take a lot of effort to catch. Many times the money trapper cannot afford to take the time needed to get these educated varmints. It is better to move to new territory and work on the ones easier to catch. Too, by leaving some brood stock in an area the trapper ensures a continuing supply of fur from the area.

When pulling the traps, pick up all pan covers and wire from the set and smooth the dirt down around the set. Leave the place clean for next year's trapping. If trapping on a ranch, tell the rancher when you leave. If someone then comes in and traps the area without permission and does damage you will not be blamed.

10
Bobcat

The bobcat is one of the easiest of the predators to trap, and if the cats are using an area, even an inexperienced trapper can take one or two. To take cats consistently, though, a trapper must know the animal and its habitat.

Bobcat are found from southern Canada to Central America, and in the United States, from coast to coast. The bobcat will vary greatly in size. A cat was taken in Colorado in 1951 that weighed 69 pounds. Cats that weighed more than 50 pounds have been reported from Nevada, New Mexico, and Ohio. This is unusually large for a bobcat, however; they generally weigh less than 20 pounds. Bobcat pelts also vary. Cats of the Northwest Coast show a nearly chocolate color, while those of the Southwestern desert are light gray to silver.

The bobcat is a night skulker for the most part, particularly in areas frequented by man. They will sometimes move about during daylight in wilderness areas. Bobcat often live in close proximity to man, but since they are almost totally nocturnal in their habits they aren't seen.

The bobcat makes its living by hunting rabbits and other rodents. If they are scarce it will eat game and nongame birds, snakes, lizards, poultry, invertebrates, grass, foxes, fish, and the young of big-game animals. It is also fond of the young of domestic livestock. It hunts in a stealthy walk and will sometimes trot. With a top speed of 15 miles an hour it is not particularly fast. It will follow the same hunting route night after night, and will have favorite sites along the course to deposit scat. A bobcat will start hunting a little before sundown and may cover 7 miles before dawn breaks. The hunting range will average about 5 miles—less than that if game is plentiful, and slightly more if times are hard. Old toms usually hunt alone. A female will often be escorted by a

Most bobcat of the Southwestern desert are light in color and have an almost pure-white underbelly marked with black spots. This big Arizona tom weighed 25 pounds. *(Photo: Gerry Blair)*

young tom, and many times will be accompanied by several half-grown kittens from the last litter.

A bobcat will spit, growl, and hiss much like a domestic cat. It will also caterwaul like a domestic tom and can be heard from a mile away during the breeding season, which usually starts the last of February and may continue through the first part of May. About two months after breeding the young are born, in a rock overhang, brush pile, or some area sheltered from severe weather. The litter will consist of two to seven kittens, with the average being two or three. The female nurses the young for about two months and then begins to teach them to eat solid food and to hunt for themselves. They will stay with the mother until early fall, and in some cases through the winter. The female is careful to hide the litter from the male bobcat, as he will kill and eat the kittens if

The long-legged bobcat has a wide color variety throughout its range. This dark specimen from West Virginia brings the trapper less money than the lighter varieties. *(Photo: U.S. Dept. of Agriculture)*

given a chance. Females who are not impregnated during the regular breeding season may come into heat later in the year. Consequently, very small kits are often caught during the trapping season. Some are no larger than small housecats. Many trappers release the kits to be taken when they have become grown the following year.

ECONOMIC STATUS
The economic status of the bobcat must be considered from a number of viewpoints. Some game-management specialists·consider it a valuable check on rodent population. Farmers and ranch-

ers dislike the bobcat because of its frequent raids upon the chicken coop or inclination for eating young calves. Sportsmen also dislike the bobcat because of its inroads into the game birds and other small game. Too, during the fawning season, the bobcat is sure to take important numbers of young deer and antelope. Its main value, it seems, is in its pelt. Bobcat fur sold for as much as $400 a pelt during the 1976-77 season, and the total catch came to several million dollars. Buyers will pay the best price for bobcat taken during December, January, and February.

TRAPS FOR BOBCAT

Bobcat are easily caught in a No. 2 or No. 3 double-spring, jump trap, or coilspring trap. Many cats have been caught in the No. 1 and No. 1½. Use the No. 2 if you can, as many larger cats will pull out of anything smaller. The No. 3 is most often used by cat trappers. There will be no pullouts and the No. 3 will also take a coyote if one happens along. The No. 2 and No. 3 jump traps are the fastest to set and easiest to conceal, so they are extensively used in combination cat and fox trapping.

The traps can be tied down, staked, or attached to a drag. A tiedown can be used if there are trees or bushes handy to serve as an anchor. Stakes can be used in open areas where no tiedowns are present. A drag can always be used. Find a limb from a tree, a rock, or one of the commercial drags available. The cat will not go far after it is trapped and fastened to a drag—probably to the nearest heavy cover where it can find a place to hide.

The bobcat is a curious animal. It is not particularly bothered by human odor around the trap sets, can easily be called by using bait, lure, or scent, and will often respond to a call scent used for a different furbearer.

READING SIGN

In selecting a trap site, consider the evidence of cat use of the area. This may be in the form of a 2-inch-diameter track in soft dirt or mud. Adult tracks resemble those of domestic cats, although they are much larger and have a different-shaped heel pad. The print will have three blunt toe projections which are indistinct claw marks. Scratches will be found where urine has been evacuated. The scat will usually be deposited just off the trail or on an elevated point. These droppings can be distinguished from fox

Animals will sometimes develop community toilets. This is scat from four separate bobcat visits. A trap set here will almost surely take a bobcat, or perhaps several. *(Photo: Gerry Blair)*

feces because bobcat scat is larger, it is more stubby at the ends, and it is often semi-segmented. Bobcat scat differs from coyote droppings in being more segmented and having blunter ends. Near a den area, bobcat will often fill a small dug-out hole with droppings. A tom bobcat often has his scenting and scratching area on the northeast side of a boulder ridge and usually visits these areas at intervals of one to two weeks.

TRAVEL HABITS
Most bobcat when leaving a large timbered area will make a beeline for the next good cover. It will leave a ridge by working off a point, and before it drops off this high place, will carefully scrutinize the land below. It will be looking for something to eat, and also for its enemy the coyote. Only a very large tom will venture into open country where it is likely to encounter a coyote.

Sand washes are followed as pathways. The walking is easier here, and the brushy sides of the wash are good cover for the rodents that make up the staple food of a bobcat. Cats that use a

This bobcat had been feeding on rabbits—the scat consists totally of hair. *(Photo: Gerry Blair)*

sand wash on a regular basis will sometimes step in exactly the same spot they used on the last trip through. Where sand washes meet, or where a rocky ridge tapers into a sand wash, every cat coming through will leave sign.

Lone piles of big boulders, large masses of downed timber, and big brush piles are visited by every cat coming through. In heavily timbered areas or marshes, bobcat will follow game trails and roads. Small open areas surrounded by timber or heavy brush are also visited on a regular basis. A bobcat will cover a set pattern when it travels its hunting course. The length of time it takes it to return to any given point will vary depending upon the availability of game. It may cover its rounds in one night, or if game is scarce, may have a hunting route that takes two or three weeks.

BOBCAT SETS

Often two cats travel together, an adult male and female. Another combination may be an adult female with last year's young tagging along. If the female is trapped, it is likely that the young will remain in the same general area. Because of these factors, having two or three sets in the same area will take extra cats.

Blind Set

In areas where a bobcat is using a trail to and from a hunting area or den, the blind set can be used successfully. A blind set is any set made without the use of scent or bait. Find where a limb, root, or rock is being stepped over. Dig in on one or both sides of the obstacle, depending on whether you intend to use one or two traps. Two trap sets double your chance of success. If you cannot find a natural obstacle being stepped over, put a small limb across the trail. If the limb still has leaves attached, so much the better. Clean off a spot on each side to set the traps. The cat will not step on the leaves if it has a choice.

The trap holes should be dug so that the trap, the pan cover, and about ¼ inch of loose dirt will not raise the area above ground level. Dig the trap holes only about an inch apart if you do not have a step-over stick. Fasten the two trap chains together with baling wire. Now wire down to a rock, a tree branch about 6 feet long, or any stationary object. If you use a stake, do not stake near the bottom of a tree. The cat will climb the tree, and the straight-up pull on the stake will cause it to pull loose.

When setting the traps, have the springs pulled slightly toward the dog of the trap to get both jaws level with the pan. Use a piece of light canvas, or a piece of waxed paper, as a pan cover. If rodents are apt to dig up the canvas, be sure to use wax paper. The cover should fit over the trap pan and under the two jaws. It should be large enough to prevent any dirt or twigs from working under the pan. The No. 2 coilspring trap is easy to set up and will easily take cats. It will also hold any fox that comes in to explore the cat set, and occasionally a coyote. When the pan cover is in place, take a dirt sifter with ¼-inch mesh and screen dirt, ground-up manure, or sand over the dug-in trap and trap chain. Cover the spring areas and chain first. Make sure the trap is well bedded.

Although cats are not usually afraid of human scent, use the same precautions here that you would in making a coyote set. Many times a coyote will come into a cat set, and sometimes a trap-wise bobcat will be scared off by a human smell. Use rubber gloves when handling the trap and the trap cover, and use a kneeling tarp while you are making the set. The traps should have been boiled, colored, and waxed. You will take an extra five or six coyote or fox every season that you would otherwise miss. This will more than pay you for your extra time.

The completed set should be left in a natural condition, free of human scent. Any loose dirt left over from digging the trap holes should be carried away from the site and scattered.

Scent-Post Set

Scents may consist of straight bobcat urine, fish oil or paste, scents made from cat glands and feces, or a commercially prepared scent. If you run only a few traps on a part-time basis, you are probably better off buying a commercially made scent, but if you devote your full attention to the trapline, you should make your own scent and lures (see Chapter 4).

When setting a scent-post set, move off the trail a foot or so. This will minimize the capture of nontarget animals. All predators have good noses and will be able to smell the scent. Place the scent on a small stick or bush about 8 inches above the ground. Use three or four drops of scent and add a drop or two about once a week. If there is a hard rain, re-scent with three or four drops, as the rain washes most of the scent away. Use two traps. Put the first trap directly between the trail and the scent post. This will catch the animal that approaches the set in a straight line. Position the other trap in a line with the scent post but 8 or 10 inches to the left or right. This will take the animal that comes to the post with the intention of leaving its own scent.

Set the traps in the same manner as in the blind set described previously. Coyote, fox, and other predators will sometimes visit a scent set for bobcat, and the careful trapper will receive a bonus in these occasional visitors. A bobcat, or any predator for that matter, will get pinched in a scent set once in a while and will escape. These trap-wise animals will not come into a set again which has the same scent. For this reason it is advisable to use more than one type of scent on your line. Even a trap-wise animal will come into a set with an unknown variety of scent.

Cubby Set

A cubby set is a set that uses scent, bait, or both, and that forces the bobcat to approach the trap in only one direction, or at most two directions. A hollow log open at both ends might be used for a natural cubby. The bait or lure would be placed in the middle of the hollow and a trap would be set at each end. Bobcat are easy to catch using bait. Sometimes all that is needed is an attractor such as the wing from a bird or small piece of rabbit fur.

Left and Above: A cubby set can be made from dead limbs. Lean the limbs out from a tree so that there is only one way in. The two traps are set on each side of a step-over stick. The bait goes on the tree at the back of the cubby. *(Photos: Gerry Blair)*

The North-Country cubby is built of whatever material is at hand. Branches, downed trees, rocks, and bark are all good. The finished cubby resembles an open-ended box or a natural shelter. The roof protects the trap and the bait from rain and snow. Best results will be obtained if the cubby is placed near a travel route. Put the bait near the back of the opening and hang it from the roof so that it is suspended above the ground. The scent will travel better and the bait will be more visible. Put the traps near the front. With only one way in, the cat has to walk across the traps to get to the bait. Another variation is to put one trap near the front of the cubby and the second trap under the bait. If the first one doesn't

Angle the traps slightly so that the widest part of the jaw is presented. Angle the pan dog away from the direction of travel. *(Photo: Gerry Blair)*

get the cat, the second one will. Sticks or rocks can be used to force the animal to step into the trap. Place a few drops of scent on a stick at the top of the cubby. For bait, tie a small piece of jackrabbit with the fur still on to the top of the cubby. Chicken, squirrel, muskrat, and beaver carcasses have also been used with good results. The jackrabbit is more of a natural food source for the cat, however, and will produce the best results if it is available. Many other furbearers will visit a cubby set for cat, including marten, fisher, wolverine, fox, badger, and skunk.

The desert cubby is usually more open at the top than the one described above. It will resemble a V-shaped pen with the point of the V ending against a rock or a tree. The bait is hung at the point of the V about 18 inches above the ground to make it more visible and to allow the wind to carry the news. Use dead limbs, rocks, or cactus segments to form the legs of the V. Place guide sticks so that the cat must step on the trap to get to the bait. Use a little scent, and throw a handful of chicken or duck feathers on the floor of the cubby. Be sure to have your bait fastened so that it is not visible from the air; eagles and hawks also like rabbit and will come into the set if they can see it from the air, and they will spring the trap and maybe cause the loss of a big bobcat. Although they are not usually seriously hurt, it is time-consuming to release them and to reset the trap.

At a cubby set, it is best to use a drag. This allows the animal to move away from the set before it has a chance to tear it up too badly. Use a rock, a dead tree limb, or a grapple for the drag.

Dirt-Hole Set

A dirt-hole set also works well for bobcat, and if properly set, will take any fox and coyote that happens by. Dig a hole about 4 to 6 inches across and about 6 inches deep. On flat ground, slant the hole into the ground at a 45-degree angle. If the hole is to be dug on a bank or on a hillside, dig straight back in. The hole is most easily dug with a hand trowel. Leave the dirt in front of the hole as though it was dug out by a predator. If you are using fresh bait, dig the hole in such a manner that the sun will not strike it. The bait will then stay fresh longer. Put the bait near the bottom of the hole and sprinkle a little loose dirt over it, or partially cover it with a handful of grass. A handful of feathers or rabbit fur at the front of the hole is a good attractor. Use a drag on the trap chain so that the animal will leave the area before destroying the set.

Set one trap about 8 inches directly in front of the hole, and set the other about the same distance to the right of the hole. Put the traps into the ground in the same manner as for the blind set. Use the same precautions in trap handling that you would in a coyote set. Dirt-hole sets are murder on coyote, and you will catch several in the traps set for bobcat. Keep the bait fresh to attract the bobcat—a cat does not usually come to tainted bait. If the weather remains warm, use fur and feathers and scent at the set rather than the bait. A squirt of cat urine on the upper lip of the hole is a good attractor on some of the sets.

KILLING THE CATCH

A trapped bobcat is 20 pounds plus of fighting fury. It is not likely to attack the trapper, as it is more concerned with getting away than in attacking. The cat will usually back up into a bush or tree as far as the chain will permit. If it is securely caught it should be stunned with a kill stick. Then strike the animal just back of the front leg with the foot or knee. This breaks the heart loose and the blood is released into the chest cavity. The pelt will then remain free of blood.

If the bobcat is not caught securely, do not attempt to kill it in this manner. It will surely pull out of the trap in its efforts to avoid the stick, and a pelt will be lost. Carry a .22 rifle or handgun on the trapline and load it with .22 Shorts for shooting animals that are not securely caught. Shoot from close range so that there will be no possibility of a miss, and aim between and a little above the eyes. The bullet will penetrate the skull and the brain but will not continue through to do more damage. There will be almost no blood, and the small hole left by the bullet will cause no damage to the pelt.

SAVE CAT URINE

Bobcat urine should be saved for later use in preparing scent-post sets. As soon as the bobcat has been killed, elevate the hind end. The sphincter muscle which controls the bladder will relax soon after death, and all urine in the bladder will be evacuated if the carcass is lying flat. Some trappers carry a plastic spray bottle with them on the line to collect and spray out the urine.

The traps should be reset and rebaited unless the trapper is convinced that the area is no longer fruitful. Rearrange the set to return it to a natural appearance. The odor left by a trapped cat may assist in bringing in another cat of the area. A well-hidden trap will take more fur and will also minimize trap theft. Take the customary precautions about leaving human scent, and do not allow any blood from the trapped animal to remain around the set.

SKINNING

If the weather is warm, the cat should be skinned as soon as possible—never more than an hour or two after death. If it's left unskinned, the digestive juices of the stomach will cause the fur along the inside of the belly to turn green. Fur buyers will check for this condition and will pay less for such poorly handled fur.

To skin a bobcat, suspend the carcass by one hind leg from a tree limb or other support. Cut the inside of one hind leg, starting at the foot and continuing to the vent. Continue on from the vent to the foot of the opposite hind leg. It is not necessary to skin out the foot and claws. Cut around the circumference of the leg at the first joint above the foot on both legs and strip the skin from the carcass. To skin out the stubby tail, use the knife to get it started. Insert the thumb and forefinger at the edge of the fur and pull the tailbone from the fur. Tail-pulling sticks may simplify this task. Pull the pelt down over the stomach and front shoulders, using the knife on stubborn areas. Continue stripping and cutting, and cut off the front leg fur just above the ankle joints. Use extreme care around the head. The skin is tight here, and the knife must be used. The ear cartilage must be cut close to the skull. Cut the membrane by the eye, the inner lips, and the nose cartilage to free the hide. Do not allow blood to stain the fur as it is being skinned.

If the bobcat is bleeding at the nose, tie a plastic bag over its head with a handful of paper towels inside. After skinning past the front legs, free the tied hind leg and with the head up, remove the plastic bag. Wipe free blood from the nose and mouth and rehang by tying the rope to the free pelt. Blood will drain back into the body of the cat and the weight of its body will make the skinning of the head easier. This also keeps the hide above and out of the dirt.

Before putting the skinned pelt on the drying board, all fat and meat tissue must be removed. The ears and the lips will have the most meat left on them. With a pocket knife, make a small slit in the tail tip. Now put a teaspoon of table salt into the top of the tail opening, and with a blunted wire force the salt down inside the tail. This prevents spoilage even in warm weather. Lightly salt around the ears and the lips. The tail of the bobcat may be totally split on the underside to ensure rapid drying instead of using salt. This method is probably used by most trappers.

CARE OF THE PELT

Some bobcat hides may be improved by washing. If the pelt is to be washed, do this before any salt is applied. Use a liquid detergent in lukewarm water. After the pelt has been washed, rinse it in clear water until all of the detergent has been removed. Washing a bobcat skin will usually make it much lighter in overall color and will cause the hair to fluff.

Put the pelt on a drying board of the proper size. Wood is preferred by many long-line trappers. Wood stretchers may be built in a variety of sizes, and a stretcher can be selected that is a close fit for the pelt (see Chapter 4). The tapered end should be slightly rounder for bobcat than for coyote.

An average-size bobcat will stretch to about 52 inches from the nose to the end of the leg skin, and about 38 inches from the nose to the end of the tail. Spread the stretcher boards so that the fur is about 8½ to 9 inches wide at the hips and about 7 inches wide at the shoulders. Nail the ends of the pelt into place on the wood to prevent movement. Stretch the pelt with the fur side in and the skin side out to allow maximum drying. When the pelt is nearly dry, remove the nails and take the pelt from the stretcher. Turn the front legs to the inside by using needlenose pliers. Now turn the entire pelt so that the fur side is to the outside. Replace the pelt on the stretching board, adjust the legs to a proper fit, and renail the skin.

If the pelt is too dry to turn easily, or the leg skins are brittle-dry, take a wet cloth or a wet paper towel and rub it along the thin edge of the pelt. Do this on both sides, and repeat two or three times in a fifteen-minute period. The pelt will loosen up and will turn easily.

Do not dry the hide in direct sunlight, to avoid possible damage to the fur and faster spoilage to any area not totally dry. Put it in a shady spot, preferably one that has good air circulation. When the pelt is thoroughly dry, check the lips and front legs to make sure they too are dry. Remove the pelt from the stretcher and hang it in a well-ventilated room with no sunlight. All furs should be cleaned of burrs, resin, and other foreign matter before being stored.

Properly skinned, fleshed, washed, dried, and stretched bobcat pelts will bring 20 to 50 percent more money from the buyer than those not properly prepared. Proper stretching is the most important element. The length and shoulder width of the pelt is a crucial measurement. Fur color and condition are also important.

RELEASE OF FEMALE
In many areas of the United States, trapping is legal from November through February, and the fur is usually prime during this period. Some female bobcats will accept the male during December and January, and will drop their kittens the following February and March. It is good business to turn a pregnant or nursing female loose, as it will surely provide extra pelts for the next year's trapping. See Chapter 6 for the proper technique.

11
Fox

The fox is a doglike predator that is widespread over most of North America. Although there are a number of species worldwide, only three of the North American species are important as a furbearer. Those three are the Arctic fox, the red fox, and the gray fox.

The Arctic fox is found in northern Canada and in Alaska; because of its range we will not discuss it in detail. It is a small fox and wears a white coat during the winter months. In summer the coat changes to gray or brown. The Arctic fox has small ears, a somewhat blunt face, and dense fur. A winter color phase of the Arctic fox is the blue fox.

GRAY FOX
The gray fox has a body length of about 2 feet, and the bushy tail extends about another foot. A large gray fox will tip the scales at about 15 pounds, but a small adult weighs half that, and they should average about 10 pounds.

The gray fox's fur is salt-and-pepper gray with a buff underfur. The sides, legs, and feet are usually rusty orange. The belly is white shading off to light orange on the sides. The tail is black-tipped and has a black stripe running its entire upper length.

The gray fox is common over most parts of the United States. About the only place it is not found is the Northwestern plains. The range extends south into South America. A smaller species, closely related to the gray fox, is found on the islands off southern California.

The gray fox breeds during midwinter, and about two months later the vixen delivers two to seven young. The kits are born in an abandoned badger hole, a large brush pile, or a slide rock area. The young venture outside of the den when they are about five weeks old. The forays are first confined to the area immediately surrounding the den, but by midsummer the young will go with the adults as they hunt, and will be taught the skills needed to exist away from the parents. If the home area has a scarcity of game, the young will leave to find greener pastures sometime in the early fall. Otherwise they are likely to set up residence in the same area in which they were born.

It is not uncommon to see a male and female hunting together during the winter months. The fox is a night hunter mostly, although it may be seen about at dusk and shortly after daylight. If times are hard and food is scarce, the fox will also hunt during daylight hours.

The fox is territorial, and the home range varies with the supply of food animals available, from about ¼ square mile to as much as 3 or 4 square miles when food is scarce. The gray fox is omnivorous—that is, will eat both meat and plant material: rodents, insects, amphibians, reptiles, birds, garbage, carrion, fruits, and berries. The gray fox is the only member of the dog family that is a tree climber. It is a good climber and will often use this ability to escape one of its natural enemies, the coyote.

RED FOX

The red fox is usually a bit larger than the gray. The coat is reddish-yellow with a white-tipped tail. The legs and feet are black. The color will vary slightly. The cross fox, the black, and the silver are all color phases of the red.

The red fox also breeds in midwinter but the gestation period is shorter than the gray's, about fifty-one days. Four to ten young are born in any den that offers privacy and protection. Like the gray, the red fox uses abandoned animal dens and other natural cubbies if they are available. If not, the red digs a den of its own.

The young will come outside the den after five weeks, and three weeks later are traveling with the parents. The young red stays with the parents until fall. Like the gray they will set up housekeeping near the birth area if game is plentiful. If not, they hit the road to find new territory.

The red fox has extended its range during the past forty years and is now found throughout most of North America. Exceptions are the arid desert land of the Southwest and the northern fringe of Canada and Alaska.

The young of the year seek out their own home range during

late fall and winter. It is likely that they will cover a lot of ground before they settle down. As with the gray fox, home-range boundaries are determined by geography and by the availability of food.

HARMFUL EFFECTS OF FOX
The red fox is more of a problem around poultry than the gray. The damage is usually caused by a single fox, and if it is trapped, the predation usually stops. If food is plentiful a fox will not come to a chicken pen as a rule. They like to keep a safe distance between themselves and the dangers of man.

Like most members of the dog family the fox is not a fussy eater; when hungry it will eat almost anything, including carrion and garbage. A hungry fox will sneak into a farmer's yard and clean out the dog's dish.

An overpopulation of fox in an area increases the chance of a rabies epidemic, and will also result in distemper and mange.

VALUE AS A FURBEARER
Fox fur has been a staple of the trapping industry for many years. The fur primes out in late October in the North Country and about the middle of November farther south. The fox begin to sun-singe about the last of January, perhaps earlier if there is an early spring. Rubbing shows up about the same time. The fur degrades rapidly from both of these conditions. The trapper is well advised to pull his traps when either condition is noticed. Fur prices for both the red and the gray fox peaked in the mid-1970s: During the winter of 1977-78, the grays brought an average of $36 and the reds an average of $55. As with other fur, the main demand appears to come from European markets.

TRAPS FOR FOX
Red and gray fox have been taken in traps ranging from the No. 1 longspring to the No. 4 wolfer. The correct-size trap to use will almost always start a heated discussion among any group of experienced trappers. Usually, the No. 1 longspring is too small to take and hold fox. If No. 2, No. 3, and No. 4 traps are used the fox is usually taken high on the leg and a broken bone may result. If caught in a single trap, a fox with a broken leg twists off rapidly. In the Southwest many fox are taken in sets made for coyote. Coyote sets usually are two-trap sets, and the fox is often caught in both

In late January or early February the fox will begin to sun-singe and rub at the hips. This red fox from West Virginia shows both conditions. *(Photo: U.S. Dept. of Agriculture)*

traps. One caught by two legs does not escape. If only one trap is used at a set, the big No. 3 and No. 4 traps will surely break the leg and the fox is more likely to twist off. It does not last long in coyote country though, as a three-legged fox is almost sure to see the inside of a coyote's belly in short order.

The No. 1 trap works well for fox and usually does not break the leg. This trap also holds other furbearers who may volunteer to the set. The trap has a disadvantage in the small size of the jaw spread. The No. 1½ longspring is often used for fox. If the fox trapping is done in country where bobcat are present, the No. 2 coilspring, the No. 2 jump trap, or the No. 2 longspring is a good choice. This size trap works well on fox and holds most of the bobcat that show up. Use two-trap sets and the few fox that would ordinarily twist out of the No. 2 will be kept.

The No. 1½ coilspring, either the new version or a reworked older model, has proved to be a top fox taker. The trap strikes low to catch the lower foot and is strong enough to hold the animal. For extensive fox trapping this trap is a top choice.

The Conibear takes very few fox. Snares can be used for fox in brushy habitat where trails are obvious through thick brush or weeds. The No. 1 snare is the main snare used for fox. To trap the fox, particularly the red fox, all traps must be cleaned, derusted, dyed, and waxed before using. The red fox is more difficult to trap than the gray. Use the same precautions in trapping the red that would be used in making a coyote set.

READING FOX SIGN

If the fox trapper does not know his territory like the back of his hand, he had better be out before the season begins to scout the area. He should watch for droppings, tracks, scent posts, scratchings, and dug-up areas where the fox has worked for rodents. Tracks will be found in the loose dust of a trail, in soft mud after a rain, in fresh snow, or along the sandy bottom of a dry wash. Fox tracks are similar to dog tracks but are smaller than most. Many times the rear imprint will overlap the front track to create a double track. The track is four-toed with a full or partial pad showing. Claw marks are usually visible on all toes.

Pocket gopher mounds are a natural for fox to scout and leave their tracks. The muddy banks of streams and lake shores will also show evidence of fox activity.

Check the junction of two or more trails, the points of ridges, and old roads for droppings and scent posts. Many times three or four separate droppings will be found indicating that fox, or a single fox, has left scent there over a period of time. Fox leave urine and offal at a place where another fox has evacuated. They do the same on top of bobcat scat. If one of these community toilets is found, the trapper is almost sure to catch an animal there. Passes between two ridges, fence corners, and the forks of a sand wash are likely spots to find fox sign.

The fox often follows the game trails along a ridge top. It seems to be more of a high hunter than its cousin the coyote. If there are large numbers of coyote present the fox numbers tend to be lower. The fox has a tough time competing with the coyote for food, and the coyote makes a meal of the fox at every opportunity. A fox in coyote country usually sticks to the high ridges or the brush.

The droppings of the fox are somewhat like coyote droppings but slenderer, and tapered on the ends. An inspection of the droppings shows what the fox has been eating. Hair in the droppings indicates rodents or carrion. Prickly pear turns the droppings an off-red color, and many seeds will be seen. When the trapper knows what the fox is eating he can locate feeding areas and place traps in those locations.

SETS FOR FOX

Set-making tools are the usual ones—dirt sifter, rubber gloves, wire, pliers, stakes and drags, a kneeling pad, pan covers, fox lure, chunk bait (see Chapters 3 and 4). Fox urine is very helpful. If the area trapped contains both red and gray fox, use the urine from the red. The red fox is much harder to trap than the gray and might not come to a trap scented with gray-fox urine. The gray is less particular and is not afraid of the red.

Dirt-Hole Set

The old reliable dirt-hole set usually brings more fox hides to market than all the other types combined. The fox does a lot of natural digging to get its grub and will explore most of the fresh-dug holes it comes across. Too, it is an opportunist. If it believes that another animal has buried something of interest, it is sure to explore.

Select a trap site that is beside a trail used by fox, to the side of a little-used road, a sandy wash, or the sloped bank of a stream. These are all locations where a fox, or another predator, might bury a tasty snack. When the location has been chosen, put all necessary equipment in the pack basket and walk directly to the spot. Put the kneeling tarp on the ground in front of the set and stand or kneel on it to minimize the amount of human scent left at the set. Use the long-handled trowel to dig a hole about 4 inches wide and 8 inches deep. Back the hole with a tuft of grass, a low bush, or a low rock. The backing will prevent the fox from coming into the hole from the back side. The backing, however, should be low enough that the fox can see over it with no trouble. The size, slant, and depth of the hole do not have to be exact. A small hole is suggested because it is easier and faster to prepare. A large hole would do as well but would take longer to prepare.

The traps should be positioned so that the fox will hit the trap pan with a front foot when its nose is at the edge of the bait hole. Put the traps back about 6 inches from the lip of the hole. If one trap is used, put it on the right side of the hole about 6 inches back. If two traps are used, put the second slightly to the left of the first trap and about 2 inches farther back from the hole. Animals, like humans, seem to be mostly right-footed. When they stand to investigate the bait hole they will usually hold the right foot slightly forward of the left. Most animals, when caught by a front foot, will spring the trap with the right foot rather than the left. Put the free jaw of the trap to the left of center. If two traps are used, put the free jaw of the second trap toward the center of the hole also. If a stake or drag is used, drive or bury it before the traps are positioned. The traps will be placed over the buried tiedown with as little disturbance of the site as possible. Bed the trap well, and put a small rock under the free jaw of the trap so that loose dirt under the jaw will not cause the trap to shift when it is stepped on. Put dirt inside the spring openings if longspring traps are used. The coilspring traps are easier to dig in and conceal; they are smaller and require less hole. Wax-paper pan covers with a 2-inch slit cut out for the pan dog work well. Some trappers use a cloth pan cover; they can boil the cloth with local aromatic herbs or tree limbs to impart a strong local scent that will help to disguise any trap odor. But rodents are often a problem whenever cloth pan covers are used.

Cover the traps by screening dirt over them. Cover the spring areas first and then the center. When the set is covered it should be level with the surrounding ground. Finish off the set by using a small stick to make the ground above the trap look natural. The dirt covering the trap should be ¼ to ½ inch deep.

Put a thumb-sized chunk of bait to the back of the hole. The bait should be partially covered with dirt, leaves, or loose grass. This allows the fox to smell the bait but makes it hard for it to see it. A few drops of fox urine sprinkled at the upper lip of the hole often add to the set. The urine reinforces the thought that another fox has been to the set. It is a good suspicion remover for any member of the dog family. Leave the loose dirt from the hole in a mound at the hole entrance.

When the set is finished, follow the usual steps to leave the set smelling and looking natural.

Many variations of the dirt-hole set can and should be made on the trapline. Try different kinds of bait. Make the dirt holes different sizes. In wooded areas try a handful of feathers at the hole entrance.

Scent-Post Set

The fox, like other members of the dog family, leaves scent at regular locations in its territory. A lone low bush or weed is most often used. Watch for scratches along wooded roads, beside trails, and along streams or dry washes. If a natural scent post cannot be located, make one by squirting fox urine on any low bush or weed along a fox runway. This works better if it is done several weeks before trapping season.

If a well-grazed meadow is to be trapped the scent post can be made at a dry cow chip, a small stake, a fence post, or a rock.

Before placing the traps at a scent-post set, determine the direction of the prevailing wind. Place the traps so that the wind will carry the scent from the traps to the trail. Otherwise the scent will be blown away from the trail and passing fox will not pick it up. One or two traps can be used at a scent-post set. One trap will take fox, but two will take more. With one trap, set it to the right of the scent post so the pan is 4 inches from the scent. The free jaw should be to the inside and against the bush. Dig the trap in and finish off the same as a dirt-hole set.

If two traps are used—and they should be—put the second trap about 6 inches in front of the scent post with the jaws spread to the left and right. The first trap will take the bold walk-up-to-it fox and the second will take the fox that misses the first but decides to leave a little of its own liquid on the scent post.

A set that has caught a fox will probably take another. The odor and scent left by the caught fox is a good attractor for others. Push a small stick into the ground or use another cow chip at the edge of the dug-up ring made by the first fox. Put on a squirt or two of urine and reset the traps. Fox often travel in pairs, so it is likely that a second will be close by. Some trappers will make two sets in the same area in an attempt to catch both the same night.

Make a variation of the scent-post set by leaving a small piece of chunk bait or lure at the set. If the weather is rainy, tilt a dry cow chip or piece of bark to make a roof for the bait. This will let the bait or scent keep its odor longer. Add fresh scent every three or four days in damp weather.

Blind Set

The trail set can be effective where there are signs of fox travel. Look for a natural step-over in the trail. If none can be located,

To make a scent-post set, find an area being used as a scenting area. If none can be found make one from a lone clump of grass or a dead stick. Dig a hole large enough to accept the drag or stake and the trap.

Bury the drag and bed the trap above it. Fill in the springs with dirt. Adjust the pan tension so that the pan sets level with the jaws.

Put the pan cover in position and cover with a trowelful of fine dirt.

Use a small stick to tuck the pan cover under the jaws.

Use the dirt sifter to cover the trap completely. Finish the ground above the trap level to blend with the surrounding ground.

Finish off the set with fine grass. Spray fox urine on the scent post just to the left of the prime trap. *(Photos: Gerry Blair)*

make one by using a stick, a rock, or a small clod of dirt. Put the pan of the trap about 2 inches away from the step-over. Set the jaws of the trap so they are parallel with the trail. Use a drag and the set will be damaged. Too, the caught fox will pull the drag away from the trail and hide, and is not so apt to be stolen. If two traps are used here, put one on each side of the step-over.

Water Set

The fox does not hesitate to step in water. In areas of the East and Midwest, warm springs and shallow streams that do not freeze are good locations for fox sets. Put the trap or traps at the water's edge in enough water to cover. Put the bait on a stick so it is about 8 inches above the water. Use a drag so the caught fox can come back to dry land and find a bush to hide in. If the trapper wears hip boots and stays in the water when he makes the set, he leaves no odor. Such sets also take raccoon and mink if they are in the area, and in their range will even take an occasional bobcat or coyote.

Muskrat is a good bait for a water set. Trash fish, chicken parts, or a hunk of rabbit also does the job. The traps will do best if they are dug in slightly and covered with wet leaves. Make a mound that comes just above the water surface. If it appears to be a stepping place the animal will surely use it.

Do not make the set at the edge of a steep bank, as a fox hesitates to climb down a steep bank to water. A smooth shore that is nearly level with the water is the best set.

The water set can be used when the ground is frozen, making dry-land trapping difficult. The set is fast to make and lends itself to a number of variations. Use different baits, fasten the bait above the water or in the water, make the sets in marshes, warm springs, and shallow streams, or make them along a lake bed that offers gently sloping banks.

Cubby Set

The cubby set takes gray fox readily; red fox are more cautious and will come to a cubby slower. If the set is well made, however, old red can be taken also. A modified cubby with an open top and backed by a tree or a bank is a good bet.

Lean sticks or small poles against the backstop, forming a V type of pen. Put the bait a foot or so off the ground so that the wind will advertise the product. Put the trap about 8 inches forward of the bait and positioned so that the fox has to cross the trap to taste the bait. Place the two traps the same as you would in the dirt-hole set. Put one trap 8 inches out and the second about 2 feet out. Use a step-over stick just back of the second trap. Use a drag so that the first fox caught will not destroy the set. Don't spend a lot of time making a cubby for fox. It can be very rough and simple.

If trapping in snow country, build the cubby under an evergreen tree so the limbs will protect the set from new snow. If no tree is available make a roofed cubby using limbs or brush. The baited cubby takes almost any predator that may be in the area. Even though the target animal is fox, use a trap strong enough to hold any other volunteer that comes to the trap.

Mound Set

Put the mound set in an area of heavy fox traffic. Build the mounds in the summer so the fox will have a chance to become used to them before trapping season opens. Make each mound about 2 feet high and 3 feet wide at the base. When the season opens, dig in the drag and bed the trap over it. Use the top of the mound. Put the bait about 20 feet away from the mound and tie it down so it can't be dragged off. The fox will use the mound to look over the bait and will be caught. This set will prevent livestock and other nontarget animals from trampling the set.

A large anthill can be used as a natural mound. Many of these hills have a chafflike material in them that prevents trap freeze-ups in very cold weather.

Chaff-Bed Set

The chaff-bed set works well in farming areas. The set takes a lot of time to make, but if it is in an area being trapped year after year it does produce good results.

Choose an area with slightly sloping ground in a little-used weedy field. It is better if the field is near woods or heavy brush. Make a hole 4 feet across and 6 inches deep. At the low edge, dig a channel to let off any water that collects from rain. Fill the cavity with a dark-colored chaff. The chaff should completely fill the hole and come slightly above the ground level. Take the removed dirt away from the area and dump it. Bury pieces of bait in the chaff. The set works best if it is made and baited before trapping season starts. Get the fox used to coming there and good catches will be made as soon as the season opens.

When the season opens put in fresh bait near the center of the bed. Bury two or three traps about 6 inches back from the bait. Use drags on all traps, as the bed will take several fox, sometimes more than one in a single night. Both the red and the gray fox will come to a chaff bed. The chaffing material can be dried horse manure, manger chaff, or broken-up straw that was used for livestock bedding.

Campfire Set

The campfire set takes a lot of time to make but will take a smart old fox that won't come to another set. In some areas, fox dig around old campfires because they have learned that bits of food are often buried there. The trapper can make a small campfire, or if he is in an area where he does not want to make a fire, he can haul in ashes to make the set. Dig a hole about a foot wide by 4 inches deep, and dig up the ground and make it look rough for several feet out from the ashes. Bury meat scraps in the ashes. A small piece of wood or a rock can be positioned along one side of the pit. Opposite the wood or rock, dig in the traps at the very edge of the ashes. Sprinkle a few ashes over the traps. Use a drag so the caught fox will leave and will not damage the set. Some trappers make a dirt-hole or a scent-post set about 50 feet away from the campfire set. This often results in a double catch.

KILLING THE FOX

The caught fox can be killed by striking it sharply just forward of the eyes with the kill stick. Do not hit too hard, as this causes bleeding. The fox becomes unconscious from the blow. Strike it just behind the front leg with the knee or the foot. This breaks down the heart and lungs and results in a fast and painless death. Some trappers prefer to shoot all trapped animals. If so, use a .22 Short or a .22 CB. Aim between and just above the eyes. Do not chance a bite from a fox, as they may carry rabies and make it necessary for the trapper to submit to anti-rabies treatment.

Do not leave more odor than is necessary around the set. Remove the fox from the trap, using rubber gloves. If the trap has any blood on it, use a fresh trap when resetting, or at least clean the used one off by rubbing dirt or sand along the jaws. Use the same precautions in resetting that were used to make the original set.

RUNNING THE LINE

Tending a fox line is best done alone. Do not take sightseers along. Two people leave twice as much scent as one and will reduce the chance of a catch.

When checking the traps, go no closer than is necessary. A good pair of binoculars will help in checking out the sets. If a drag is used, make a closer inspection, because many times a caught animal will pull away with little ground disturbance. If the trap is along a trail, do not walk the trail to check the trap. Try to make the approach from a direction that would not be used by a fox.

SKINNING

If the trapper is running a long line, he should skin out the fox as it is collected. Keep the dead fox or the skin out of the direct sun. In the Southwest particularly, where winter temperatures are warm, the fox will soon begin to taint. The hide along the belly is the first to turn. Strong stomach acids cause the inside of the hide to turn a putrid green. It smells bad and can cause a reduced price for the pelt. Many fox are fleabags, and they also host ticks and other vermin. Spray the fox with an insect spray before skinning. If this doesn't do the job, put the fox in a plastic bag and tie the mouth of the bag shut. The spray on the hide will soon kill off the freeloaders.

To speed up skinning, chop off the front feet about 2 inches above the wrist joint. This will make the front legs easier to skin. If there was a trap wound, this prevents the fur from getting bloody as the hide is pulled down over the shoulders.

Make a cut across the inside of the hind legs from foot to anal opening. Skin the hide away from the hind legs and cut free at the ankle joint. Skin out around the anus and skin the tail away from the bone as far as it can be pulled. Tie the fox by a hind leg at a comfortable working height. Pull the tailbone out of the tail and split the tail on the underside its full length. Pull and skin the fur on down until the front shoulders are reached. Skin out the front leg stubs. Pull the hide over the head and cut the ear cartilage away from the skull. Skin out the eyes and the lips and cut the nose free.

FLESHING AND DRYING

Pull the hide onto a drying or fleshing board and remove any fat or excess flesh. If there is a heavy fat layer it must be removed. Use the fleshing beam and scraper. If none are available use a sharp pocket knife and work carefully to remove the fat. Finish by scraping with a tablespoon. Wipe the leather side with paper toweling to remove residual grease and oil. Flesh the tail out also.

The drying board for the fox should be about 4½ feet long. Make it 7 inches wide at the base and 5 inches wide at the shoulders. This will be about a foot below the tip of the board. Contour the tip so that it fits the sharp-nosed fox well. This size will fit a medium red fox or a large gray. The board must be adjusted down or up ½ inch in width to accommodate other sizes.

Put the pelt fur side in on the stretcher and nail the hind legs to the board. Pull the tail down and nail the hips and tail base neatly. If a solid stretcher is used, put in a belly board that can be removed easily. Otherwise the hide will shrink up to the board so tightly that it is difficult to remove. Store the skin in a cool dry place out of the sun until it is almost dry. Remove it from the board and reverse it so that the fur side is out. Pull the ears into the normal position. Reverse the front legs by inserting a pair of longnose pliers into the leg, grabbing onto the bottom of the leg skin, and pulling through. Tack back onto the dryer and return to the cool dry place of storage. When the skin is totally dry, remove it from the board and shake the hide to fluff the fur. Hang by the nose in a cool, dry, well-ventilated area.

12
Badger

The badger is a cousin to the weasel. It is short-necked and short-legged. The front legs are well bowed, pigeon-toed, and built close to the ground. The fur is long and gray-to-brown on the upper body, and works off to white or cream on the underbelly. A white stripe goes from between the eyes to the back of the head. Many of the badgers caught in the Southwest have a white stripe the length of the back. The feet are black, with long digging claws extending from the front feet. The cheeks are white, and there is a black spot in front of each ear.

Although it usually looks bigger, the badger is only about 2 feet long and weighs from 8 to 20 pounds. Like others of the weasel family, it is a tough fighter. If it is attacked, it will lie flat on its stomach with its legs under it and put up a big bluff. It has tough loose skin on the back and a set of strong teeth to use if necessary. Rather than pay the price needed to take a badger, most other animals, even the large predators, tend to give the badger a wide berth.

The badger is found mostly in the open deserts and prairies of western North America, from Mexico to Canada and from the upper Mississippi to the West Coast. The greatest population is at elevations of 3,000 to 5,000 feet. Badgers have been trapped, however, at altitudes of 10,000 feet.

The badger has the disposition of a junkyard dog: mean and surly. But in late summer the badger will clean up his act long enough to find a mate. He advertises by leaving gland odor at selected points during his nightly traveling. When a willing partner is located, mating takes place with a lot of growling and fighting. The female carries the implanted male sperm until late winter, and at that time, the sperm will fertilize the egg. Six weeks later, one to five young are born in an underground burrow.

The badger is a fast digger; it depends on its digging ability

The badger's front claws are for digging, not defense. They have been known to outdistance a strong man with a good shovel. *(Photo: Bill Musgrove)*

and a keen sense of smell to keep its stomach filled. In soft dirt or frozen ground, the badger can easily outdistance a man with a shovel. Its claws are not used for defense, but for digging only.

The badger is a nomad, constantly on the move, and always hungry. The home range is covered thoroughly once a month or oftener. Weather, food availability, and human competition often change a set forage pattern.

The badger may have a main den. More often several holes are used for temporary dens, or wherever the animal ends up after a busy night of digging. Badgers always check out old dens to see if another animal has taken up residence there. If one has, the badger invites it to supper and the visitor is the main course, unless it is another predator. The badger will not pick fights with smaller carnivores.

The badger is a meat eater for the most part. The diet includes all of the small rodents, as well as rabbits, young birds, insects, berries, plants, worms, reptiles, and carrion.

The badger assists in controlling rodent populations. It will leave plenty of sign in prairie dog towns. The coyote and the bobcat learn quickly that the badger is no easy meal. It is a common practice for them to hunt with the badger. The badger will often be digging out a ground squirrel or a prairie dog and the animal will make a quick exit out the back door. Often there is a coyote or a bobcat waiting at the back door and the critter ends up seeing the inside of a coyote stomach rather than a badger stomach.

Badger do little harm to man. They may occasionally dig into a dirt dam at a water tank and cause a loss of water. At other times their large holes may present a hazard to livestock. For the most part, however, badger do more good than harm. They seldom come in contact with humans and are not an important transmitter of rabies. They do carry a good load of ticks and fleas. Before skinning, the trapper will probably want to give the fur a going-over with a can of insecticide.

VALUE AS A FURBEARER

The badger's fur is prime from about November until the last of February. The exact dates in specific areas will vary as the elevation changes. Yearly weather cycles will also determine primeness; an early cold winter will cause the fur to prime quicker, while a late winter causes furbearers to be slower in getting their winter coat. The value of a badger skin varies greatly; from as high as $40 or $50 some years to too little to bother with other years. Most money trappers do not spend a great deal of time trapping the badger because of the uncertain market. Too, badger are antisocial animals and will be very scattered over much of their range. Most badger taken are volunteers that come to a trap set for coyote, cat, or other animals. The long, strong digging tools of the badger, its claws, are extensively used in making Indian and Western-type jewelry.

TRAPS FOR BADGER

No. 3 trap is about right, coilspring, underspring, or longspring. Badgers are sometimes taken and held in smaller traps, but it is such a strong animal that it will often pull out. Stake the trap with a 20- to 24-inch stake if the ground is soft. If a drag is used, make sure that it is large enough that it cannot be pulled into a hole; otherwise the trapper may find himself an unwilling contestant in a digging race with a badger. Badgers are not ordinarily afraid of human scent, but if the trap is set in a place where it might take a coyote, use the same care that you would at a coyote set.

BADGER SIGN

Badger sign, for the most part, consists of locating mounds and holes dug by the badger. In snow and sand and in dusty areas, the track will sometimes resemble the coyote track. A closer inspection will usually show the claw marks on the front feet, and inside the front foot track the smaller imprint of the hind foot.

The badger is curious and always hungry. Even if it has just filled its belly it will check all of the old badger holes it comes across. This makes it an easy animal to take. If a badger is caught in a set that was made for another furbearer, it will likely ruin the set before the trapper arrives to collect it or to turn it loose. To a badger, safety is below ground, and it will dig a large mound of dirt out as far as the chain will reach.

SETS FOR BADGER

If a fresh badger hole can be located, do not set the traps directly in front of the hole. If a badger happens to be in that hole, it will back out when it leaves, kicking dirt as it comes. If the trap is directly in front of the hole it will be covered and will let the badger through without a catch. Put the traps about 6 inches to one side of the hole and about a foot back from the opening. Use bait or scent to bring the badger to the set.

The small dirt-hole set also takes badger, as well as any coyote or bobcat that may wander by. Fox also come readily to the dirt-hole set. Make a hole about 3 inches in diameter and 6 to 10 inches into the ground. Position the hole in front of a rock or a small bush so that the animal can only approach from one direction. Use lure, chunk bait, or fish oil inside the hole and cover it with a handful of grass or fine brush so that the lure will be hidden. Use two traps, No. 3 size, for the best results. Put one trap 6 inches in front of the hole and the other the same distance away but slightly to the right of the hole opening. If a stake is used, drive the stake into the trap hole before placing the traps. Finish off the traps as you would with a coyote set—that is, covering the pan, sifting dirt over the traps, and leveling the ground.

Any of the cubby sets with bait will catch badger. They are not the least bit reluctant to enter any natural or prepared cubby for a meal. Bill Ross, an outstanding coyote trapper of eastern Oregon, has caught over fifty badger in a single winter while trapping coyote using scent-post sets only.

When a badger has been caught, and has either been killed or released, the trapper has some work ahead of him in remaking the set. Use a shovel to level the mound of dirt the badger dug up. A deep hole resembling a ring, sometimes 6 feet across and 2 feet deep, will have been dug out to the length of the trap chain. Put the set back into the same condition that it was before the catch. If that is not possible, it might be easier to move the set to another location.

RELEASING

If the current price of badger fur is low, the trapper will not want to kill and keep the animal. Badgers are usually fat and are tough to skin. It takes more time to flesh and dry the hide properly. If the animal is not seriously hurt it should be released.

To release a trapped badger, use a 4-foot-square piece of blanket, a tarp, or a coat. Pull the badger away from the hole it has dug by pulling on the chain. Cover the badger's head and trapped front foot. Step on the trap spring or springs and the badger will pull its foot away from the trap. It will lumber away as fast as its bow legs allow.

A badger caught by a hind foot can usually be released by letting it crawl into a hole. Press down on the spring or springs and it easily pulls its foot out.

KILLING

If the badger is to be kept, use the killing stick to give the animal a good lick across the forehead. If it has backed deep into the hole and the ground is frozen, it will probably be best to shoot the animal with a .22 Short. Aim at the upper forehead. There will be little pelt damage and almost no bleeding.

The badger can bite severely if it gets half a chance. Don't get careless with bare hands around its face.

Transport the badger by placing it on its back in the vehicle. It will bleed less in this position and strong urine will not be released; the fur will stay cleaner, and the vehicle will not be smelled up.

SKINNING

Badgers can be case-skinned or blocked. Some fur buyers prefer one way over the other, but most will accept either method al-

This badger has been skinned open. Most buyers now prefer to buy cased badger. (Photo: Gerry Blair)

though they may well venture some advice on how to do the job the next time around.

To block, or skin open, lay the badger on its back and make a knife cut from the tip of the chin back across the belly to the anal opening. On male badger cut around the penile opening on the stomach area very carefully. Use care in cutting around the anal glands to prevent cutting into the scent glands. Continue the cut on down to the tip of the tail.

Starting from the forward edge of the pad of each foot, split the hide up the inside of the leg until the stomach cut is reached. Cut the hide loose at the wrists and give a sharp pull to jerk the leg hide away from the muscle and loose body fat. Continue pulling and cutting until the hide is off the body. It is a general practice to rough-skin the badger first and flesh the hide later.

Nail the hide, flesh side out, to a board and it will be easy to flesh. A 2 x 3-foot piece of plywood makes a good fleshing and tacking board. An old door or a shop wall can also be used. Shingle nails do the quickest job, and should be about 1½ to 2 inches apart all the way around the hide.

To flesh, start at the sides. Use a putty knife that has been reworked to have a sharp rounded end. A little experience will enable the trapper to flesh a badger in fifteen or twenty minutes. Leave the hide tacked until it is well dried. Take a paper towel to wipe down the hide and clean it free of fat.

When two or more badger pelts have been skinned, fleshed, and dried, put them on a flat surface. Put the hides flesh side to flesh side and with several thicknesses of newspaper between the hides. The paper will absorb any extra grease.

Case-skinning a badger is more work. Split the insides of the hind legs from the pad to the anal opening. Skin both hind legs free. Tie the carcass to an overhead support at a good working height. Tie by either hind foot. Split out the tail and carefully skin around the anal opening. Use the knife to peel the hide away from the body. Cut the hide loose at the wrist joints of the front legs. Continue skinning to the ears, and cut the ear cartilage free and skin around the eyes. It is faster to rough-skin the badger and then flesh it. Use a fleshing beam made for raccoon or coyote. Remove all extra flesh and fat with the fleshing knife or tool. Use a stretcher similar to a coyote stretcher but shorter (see Chapter 4). Stretch and tack into position with the fur side in. When the skin is almost dry, remove and reverse the pelt and place it back on the stretching board. Brush the fur so that it will fluff or stand out better. Some trappers place the stretcher upside down, nose to ground, so the fur will fluff better. When the pelt is dry, hang it in a cool and well-ventilated area.

The carcass of the badger will often take coyote. Put the carcass down into an old badger hole and make the set as you would for any dirt-hole set.

13
Skunk

There are four different kinds of skunk in the United States: striped, hooded, spotted, and hognosed. The striped skunk is found from central Canada to the northern part of Mexico. The spotted skunk is found throughout most of the United States. It alone of the skunks has the ability to climb. The hognosed and all hooded skunks are found through the southwestern United States and Mexico. The fur of the hognosed skunk is black except for the white back and tail. The striped and hooded skunks are black with a white stripe or stripes running from the head back onto the tail. The spotted skunk is spotted, white on black. All of the skunks except the spotted are about the size of a housecat. The spotted is smaller, about squirrel-size.

All of the skunks have the ability to discharge an offensive odor from glands located near the base of the tail. The glands are on each side of the anal opening. Fluid can be ejected in a fine spray with good accuracy up to about 12 feet. If the wind is strong the scent can be carried much farther. The scent gun is a repeater. The skunk can usually fire four to six volleys before it runs out of scent. The scent has an oil base and will remain in the scented area for a period of months. A few drops may be smelled downwind for a mile or more.

The skunk breeds in early spring and has a gestation period of about two months. The average litter is five but may go as high as twelve. Most of the skunks survive. Highways will take a few, and the great horned owl will take a few more. Mostly, though, the predators look for a meal that has a better smell.

The skunk is mainly a night feeder, although it will often be seen about during daylight. It seems to know that it carries a special immunity that allows it to go where it pleases when it pleases. Old badger holes, bankside beaver holes, woodchuck

The spotted skunk is the smallest of the skunk family. If properly handled its pelt will bring a good price. *(Photo: Gerry Blair)*

holes, crevices in rocks, hollow logs, large brush piles, and holes under buildings are common den sites for the skunk. They may travel alone or as a family group. In the winter they will often bunch up into several family groups in a single den. A den was dug out in central Montana that contained twenty-seven skunks.

The skunk may travel only a few hundred yards from its den to forage, or may go several miles, depending upon the availability of food. They eat plants, berries, fruit, insects, worms, amphibians, reptiles, birds, and mammals. They also have a taste for garbage. In rural areas and cities, they will often clean out a dog or cat dish that carries a bit of leftover food. A hooded skunk of northern Mexico was once observed to kill and subsequently eat a 3-foot rattlesnake.

HARMFUL EFFECTS

The skunk's appetite for mice, rats, and insects makes it a friend to many farmers. At the same time it does quite a lot of damage by eating the eggs and young of nesting waterfowl and other game birds, and taking a chicken whenever the opportunity presents itself. A skunk can do damage to a beehive by scratching on the hive at night. The bees exit to protect the hive and the skunk suppers on fresh bee. This continues until a hive is cleaned out.

Skunks are the primary cause of rabies in wildlife hosts. A study completed in 1976 showed that the skunk accounted for 54 percent of all diagnosed rabies in the United States. Bats were second at 27 percent, and other animals shared the remaining 19 percent. The skunk trapper provides a valuable service by preventing overpopulations and possible rabies epidemics.

VALUE AS A FURBEARER

The pelt of the skunk is always in demand by the fur industry. The market value of the skins will vary from a low of $2 to a high of $11 or $12. This is certainly a price that makes it worth the trapper's time to trap and handle the fur.

Many skunk are caught as nontarget animals in traps set for other furbearers. Some trappers will kill the animal and throw the carcass away without trying to salvage the fur. This is a waste of a natural resource. The fur and the scent can both be sold if the trapper takes the time to handle the skunk correctly. The scent serves as a base for many animal lures and scents.

TRAPS FOR SKUNK

The No. 1 longspring and the No. 1½ underspring are good traps for skunk. So is the No. 1½ coilspring. Skunk are not strong and do not fight the trap to any great extent. The smaller killer traps will also do the job. When caught in a killer trap, the skunk will seldom release scent and the fur will be easier to handle. Skunk traps do not have to be specially treated to take skunk but must work properly.

Skunks are easy to trap and can be taken in good numbers if they are about. The trap should be staked or tied to a drag that weighs 6 to 12 pounds. A lighter drag will hold a skunk, but if a fox or raccoon volunteers to the trap the heavier weight will be needed. The stake, if used, should be 14-to-18 inches long in case a larger furbearer is caught.

SKUNK SIGN

The track of the skunk is easy to recognize. The front and back feet are the same size, about 1 inch long and ¾ inch wide. There will be about 6 inches between tracks. Their step is short and they walk at an angle, leaving tracks at a 45-degree angle as they go down a trail. The pad and the toes will show in the imprint and the claws of the front foot will be longer than on the back foot.

Skunk also leave other sign. They will dig small holes around brushy canyons, near marshes, around old buildings, and in rocky areas. Watch for holes that have about a cupful of dirt removed. These are feeding areas; the skunk is digging for insects or larvae. Small boards, rocks, and dry cow manure turned over will all tell of the presence of a skunk. Close to a den, the trapper will find many slender droppings about ½ inch in diameter and about 2 or 3 inches long. Skunk scent left after a defensive encounter will sometimes be smelled. Skunks usually return to or come to a good habitat and use the same den holes year after year.

SETS FOR SKUNK

Three sets are commonly used to take skunk: the den-hole set, the bait set, and the dirt-hole set. Skunks moreover can also be taken in blind trail sets.

Den-Hole Set

The den hole might be located under a building, in a rock slide, or in a natural hole. Set one trap at the entrance and put another trap about 6 inches to the right of the entrance. The skunk will walk into an uncovered trap, but the trapper will get better results by digging in and covering the trap as he would for any other furbearer. Stakes should be driven as far back from the hole entrance as possible. If a drag is used, it should be wired to center so that the animal cannot pull it into the hole. To pull a skunk away from a building or into a box or sack, use a drowner slide on a telephone wire or old clothesline. Stake the trap end of the wire solid at the set. Run out 12 or 15 feet of wire and tie to a rock or other weight. This will keep the skunk out in the open and it can be pulled to a convenient place for killing.

If the skunk is to be released, the trapper can pull it into a box or sack. The skunk will not release scent when it is so confined; it can be moved to a desired location and released. Some trappers drown or use carbon monoxide to kill the skunk when it is so boxed. This prevents the release of scent and the contamination of the fur.

Bait Set

A bait set for skunk should do more than catch skunk if it is to pay its way. Make the set in a manner that might attract other furbearers, even though its primary target is the skunk. The main bait set used will be the full or modified cubby set. A full cubby is a natural or contrived shelter large enough to accommodate the target animal. A bait is placed near the back and traps are set at the entrance. For skunk, make the cubby about 8 inches wide, 8 inches high, and about 1 or 2 feet long. The cubby can be built against a rock or a bank. Use brush, rock, or dead limbs for the walls and the roof. Leave one end open so the animal can enter. Fasten the bait to the back end. The roof of the cubby protects the bait and traps from rain and snow, and forces the animal to enter only from the end with the traps. Use a drag and the caught animal will be less likely to tear up the set. If baits are illegal in the area being trapped, use fish oil as a lure. If baits are allowed, use chunk bait—any meat such as rabbit, birds, or fish.

A simple cubby can be made by leaning sticks against a large rock or stump, a log, or a dirt bank. Put the bait or lure at the back end and the traps at the front, and cover the trap pan with a pan cover or leaves. Make the set look as natural as possible. Fix the entrance so that the animal must step on the trap to get to the bait. Use a stepping stick if needed. The large limb used as a step-over stick may do double duty as a drag. A rock that forms the side of the cubby may also be used as a drag or tiedown.

Dirt-Hole Set

The dirt-hole set should be used in an area where there is evidence of skunk digging for grubs and mice. Make a hole in the ground a few inches in diameter and about 8 inches deep. Put lure or bait at the back of the hole. If the bait used is chunk bait, place loose grass over the bait to hide it and still let the smell come through. If a piece of meat or a piece of a dead animal is used, stake the bait to the bottom of the hole so that it cannot be easily pulled out. Set the trap several inches back from the lip of the hole and an inch or two off center. Stake and cover the trap in case animals other than the skunk volunteer. If the area shows a lot of skunk activity make three or four of these sets fairly close together.

Trail Set

A trail set made where skunk are traveling to and from feeding areas will pick up extra fur. Use a drag so that the caught animal will pull away from the trail. A limb 4 or 5 feet long and 2 or 3 inches in diameter will be about right. Use the drag as a step-over stick and place the trap or traps so that the animal's foot will trip the pan. Use pan covers. kneeling tarp, and rubber gloves, and make the set natural. The skunk won't necessarily appreciate the extra effort, but the trail set is likely to take a fox or a coyote and the extra effort will pay off in bonus animals.

KILLING

Some care is needed to kill the trapped skunk without paying the price. The skunk will almost always spray when it is killed. If the spray gets on the trapper he will probably sleep in the woodshed for a week or two. Even if the spray misses the trapper, the skunk fur will be saturated with the spray, and this will mean extra work in the fur handling. If the animal is struck in the head with the killing stock it will always spray, and it will also spray if shot in the head. The best results—and the least stink—will probably be obtained by shooting the skunk with a .22 caliber Short, or with a .22 CB, about an inch back of the front leg. A pellet gun or a BB gun might also be used. Make sure the bullet goes behind the front leg into the lung area. Do not shoot through the shoulder or into the stomach area. The low velocity of the projectile will not usually alarm the skunk; it will ignore the wound. As the chest cavity fills with blood the skunk will get drowsy, and in two or three minutes, will lie down and quietly die. This killing method usually takes less than five minutes and will rarely produce the discharge of scent.

If you are catching a lot of skunk you might prefer to construct a killing noose for the skunk. Use a $5/16$-inch-diameter steel tube about 5 feet long with a small steel cable or nylon string attached. Make a noose at the end of the tube. Put the noose over the skunk's head and pull the string tight against the neck. The animal will soon suffocate and will rarely release scent.

If the trap set is near water the skunk, still in the trap, can be dragged to the water and drowned. Any scent released is washed away by the water.

THE BIG STINK

Most trappers with lots of experience and background will have been on the wrong end of a skunk volley once or twice. If the scent hits the face or eyes, wash it off with soap and water as soon as possible. If no water is available, use snow. If the scent gets in the eyes it will sting and it should be removed as soon as possible. Keep flushing the eyes with water. The scent is an oil and will float away with the water.

If the scent hits the hands or arms it can be removed quickly by washing the affected area with gasoline. This will remove the scent. Use soap and water immediately to remove the gas. The scent can be taken from clothing in the same way. Wash the clothing with gas, lay it in a well-ventilated place to let the gas evaporate, and then wash it.

When the skunk throws scent and pollutes its own fur, it can also be removed with gasoline. Carry an empty gallon bucket in the vehicle and a container of gasoline. Place the unskinned skunk in the container and pour the gas over it. Keep pouring until the gas almost covers the skunk. Pour the gas back into the carrying container and lay the skunk aside to air-dry. Later the pelt can be washed to remove any gasoline scent from the fur. If the trap set is to be reused, do not leave any gas around the set. Take the skunk away from the set a short distance before cleaning. If the skunk must be transported before all of the gas has evaporated from the fur, use a small plastic bag to hold it.

SKINNING

Skunk are usually easy to skin. Split the inside of the rear legs from the pad to just forward of the anal opening. Cut the hide loose from each hind foot just above the pad, and use a sharp knife or surgical scissors to cut from the front of the anal opening to the outside of both scent papillae. Cut on around to the base of the tail. Pull the loose hide away from the tail base and *do not* press the scent-gland areas. Cut down the underside of the tail and remove the tailbone. Tie a small rope to a hind foot and hang the skunk at a good working height. The pelt is easily removed from the body by pulling down on the tail and hind-leg straps. Cut the hide free at the front wrists, cut the ear-base cartilage, and skin out the head.

COLLECTING SCENT

Trappers who catch many skunk will often collect the scent from the glands. The scent can either be sold to large lure manufacturers or used to make homemade scents and lures. Use a hypodermic syringe and needle with a capacity of 2 or 5 cubic centimeters. The syringes and needles are carried by most drugstores over the counter in states where that is legal, and are otherwise available by prescription. Insert the needle through the gland membrane and draw out all of the scent, then repeat on the opposite gland. Transfer the scent to a 1- or 2-ounce bottle that can be tightly sealed. Store the scent in the trapping-supply refrigerator. Clean the syringe and needle by drawing in gasoline, then soapy water. Rinse and store for future use.

FLESHING AND STRETCHING

Before fleshing, remove all burrs, tangles, and other matts that may cause the fleshing knife to grab and tear. Pull the hide over a stretching board made to fit the skunk, with the hair side in and the flesh side out. Use a knife or a scraper to work off the fat and excess tissue. If the hide has absorbed grease from the fleshing and blood from the killing, wash it in cool water to remove the blood and then in warm soapy water to remove the grease. Hang the washed pelt in a well-ventilated spot to dry. The fur side should be out so the fur will dry rapidly. When the fur has dried it is ready to be stretched.

The average-size skunk, except the spotted skunk, will need a board 3 feet long, 9 inches wide at the base, and 6 inches wide at the shoulders. It is a timesaver if boards are made that vary an inch both ways from these dimensions in order to accept larger and smaller pelts.

Stretch the skunk with the fur in. Pull the hide down on the board until it is tightly stretched. Tack each leg in place. Pull the tail area down, spread it, and tack it in place. Return to the stomach area and tack down the edges of the leg skin to make a neat and smooth stretch. Depending on humidity the pelt will dry in four or five days; in colder climates drying may take as much as two weeks.

Do not remove the hide from the board until it is totally dry. Check the lips, eyes, and base of the ears—these are the last areas to dry.

If you have trouble removing the pelt from the board, you can drill a 1-inch hole in the bottom of the stretcher. Place the hole over a spike or nail driven into a solid object and pull hard on the fur. If it still won't come, place a wedge that tapers from ⅛ inch at the nose to a little over an inch at the hips inside the pelt between the hide and the board. It is easy to remove such a wedge from a dry pelt, and the gap left makes it easy to remove the skin.

Skunk are sold with the fur in. Hang the dry pelt in a well-ventilated spot, out of the sun, until it is to be shipped.

14
Muskrat

The muskrat is widely distributed and is plentiful in many areas. It is not a true rat. It is more closely related to the field mouse, and through evolutionary changes has adjusted to an aquatic habitat. The body is about a foot long, and the hairless tail extends another 10 inches or so. An adult weighs about 2 pounds. The body is covered with a rich brown hair. The long guard hairs are coarse and glossy, and the underfur is dense and silky. The stomach area may be a grayish brown that grades off to silver.

The front feet of the muskrat are used for holding and digging. The hind feet are larger, have longer toes, and are not webbed. The toes of the hind feet have specialized hair along both sides. This allows the muskrat to use the toes much like a paddle when it swims. The chisel-like front teeth and the lips are specially adapted to permit underwater feeding. The muskrat has two musk glands near the anal opening. The glands enlarge during the breeding season, which occurs in the spring. The glands release an amber fluid at selected points in the muskrat's territory. Other muskrat visit these scent posts during the breeding season and also leave scent.

The muskrat breeds in early spring. A month later, six to eight young are born in a prepared nest. The nest will be located in an old muskrat lodge or a dug-out hole under the bank. The young are hairless and blind at birth. A week later a thin fur covering appears, and the eyes open at two weeks. A week later the young leave the nest for short exploratory trips near the nest; they are weaned at this time and will be totally independent when about five weeks old. The same female normally has another litter a month after the first. The breeding cycle continues through August, and in some parts of the United States may last through September. A female may have as many as five litters each year,

The muskrat will have feeding areas in the cattails that he visits regularly.
(Photo: Gerry Blair)

and some litters may number twelve kits. One pair of muskrat, obviously, can repopulate a community in short order.

The muskrat is mainly found in freshwater marshes, lake shores, rivers, and lazy streams. The East Coast and the Southeast coastal areas of the United States have many brackish marshes populated with muskrat. The main food of the muskrat, in fresh water, is the cattail. They will also eat bulbs, pond weed, bulrushes, horsetail, grass, roots, wild rice, and willow buds and shoots. If a shortage of plant foods develops during a hard winter, the muskrat will turn to fish, clams, insects, and frogs.

The muskrat begin building their lodges in the fall, as nights become longer and the colder temperature stimulates work activity. The lodge is the main protection against the cold of winter and the predators that like to eat muskrat; it puts a distance of water or ice between it and its enemies.

The lodge is made from plant material and mud. Often a mass of material is stacked 3 feet high and 4 feet wide at the base. One or more holes leave the lodge below the water or ice level. The living chamber is higher, at the center of the lodge. The lodge is constantly repaired and modified. Shortly after the water freezes, the muskrat will build air holes and feeding stations a short distance from the lodge. These push-ups may be found as far as 100 yards away from the lodge. They are identified by the small mounds of wadded roots and mud used to cover the openings.

The bank holes are dug from below water level and up under the bank. The den chamber is usually a foot or more above the water level and is lined with shredded plant material. Bank dens are found along small rivers and lakes.

The muskrat is found from Alaska to northern Mexico and from the East Coast of the United States to the West Coast. Unlike some other furbearers, advancing civilization has done little to affect the muskrat distribution. Civilization, in many cases, extends the range of the water rat; as dams, reservoirs, waterholes, and irrigation ditches are constructed the muskrat moves into the new territory with gusto.

Although the muskrat is mainly a water animal, and will not normally be found far from water, it will occasionally travel overland to seek out new habitat. This occurs during the high water of spring when muskrats are at their breeding peak and ground cover is plentiful. Muskrat may be found miles from the nearest water when this wanderlust strikes.

Shortly after 1900 the muskrat was introduced into Europe. It has adapted and prospered there, increasing its European range, and has started toward Asia.

Man is probably the muskrat's greatest predator. The mink lives in the same habitat and has a taste for muskrat, but probably takes an insignificant number of the total population. The mink does most of its muskrat hunting in the winter, when the prey can't get away and food is scarce. The young are extensively killed during summer months. Snapping turtles, large bass, and pike also take a few, mostly young. The land predators eat muskrat when they come ashore. The great horned owl is about the only flying predator that takes any great amount of muskrat.

The muskrat population appears to be cyclic, peaking about every seven years. Disease, reproduction success, and food availability probably contribute to the highs and lows.

The muskrat has few bad habits that annoy its human neighbors. It will occasionally dig a hole through the dirt bank of a small dam, causing water loss. If a garden is located close to a stream or a marsh the rat may help itself to a few fresh vegetables. For the most part, however, it is a good neighbor.

VALUE AS A FURBEARER

The muskrat is the main furbearer of North America, both in numbers and in total fur value. Both the United States and Canada have researched the muskrat extensively and by gaining knowledge have managed to improve and extend the muskrat habitat. Realistic trapping controls have permitted a generous harvest without decreasing total yearly numbers.

The muskrat is of value to man because of its thick silky fur. The annual harvest in the United States and Canada totals several million dollars. The income to the small trapper is important; many trappers depend on muskrat trapping to supplement the meager income they make from farming or other pursuits.

Muskrat fur is sold under its own name and as "Hudson Seal." Clothing made from the fur is durable and warm. It is also uncommonly handsome. Some restaurants buy the muskrat carcass to feature it as swamp rabbit on the menu. The meat is dark and has a rich flavor.

Muskrat pelts are prime in November in its northern range and stay prime until March or April. The southern rats prime out in December and stay prime until late February or early March.

The prime time, of course, is largely dependent upon the weather. Unprime muskrat should not be taken no matter the season. The rats will bring a low price and a valuable fur resource will be cheapened. Fur prices peak about spring.

Do not trap an area until the colony population cannot renew itself. Leave enough brood stock for reproduction and the colony will produce muskrat for many years' trapping.

MUSKRAT SIGN

Preseason scouting pays off for muskrat. Cover the area by boat or walk the lake or stream banks. Watch for runways that lead from the water into feeding areas. In marshy areas be alert for old rat houses and new ones under construction. Feeding posts where roots and tubers have been eaten will roughly indicate the number of muskrats in the area. The droppings are ratlike and will be seen on small raised areas at the edge of the water and on protruding rocks, poles, stumps, and board ends.

Check the banks for den holes. If the water is clear the holes can be seen just below the water surface. A smooth area underwater will often tip off the trapper that a lot of muskrat activity is taking place there. If there are livestock in the area they will step on the tunnels occasionally and break through. Look for plugs made with mud and reeds or grasses in these holes. If the muskrat is still in the area the holes will be plugged.

Watch muddy water channels that lead from pond to pond, or channels that lead from a bank area out to cattail feeding areas. Muskrat tracks are often seen in the soft mud along the bank. The hind foot is about 3 inches long and is V-shaped. The front foot is much smaller, about ½ inch across, and is more rounded. The front foot track will be in back of and to the inside of the hind track. The zigzag line left between the tracks is caused by the dragging tail.

The muskrat is mostly a night feeder. It will begin to feed at dusk and will finish up shortly after dawn. Watch the open water of a shallow lake, stream, or marsh at dusk and daylight and you will see muskrat feeding and working. The dens, feed areas, rest points, and travel routes can be located.

Check feeder streams entering a marsh, a canal, or a larger stream. These are always hotspots for muskrat activity. When working a drain canal in a marsh, look for tunnel holes through the banks. Watch for slides. Toilet stations or feed areas will also be easy to find.

Do not ignore other furbearers that inhabit the swamp with the muskrat. Look for raccoon, fox, mink, and skunk sign. The trapper must train himself to see and understand all of the evidence left by the target furbearers. The more he knows about the animals and their habits the more successful his trapline will be.

TRAPS AND EQUIPMENT
Muskrat trapping methods vary as habitat and climates change. The trapper should have an idea of the number of traps needed

from his estimate of muskrat populations based on preseason scouting.

Hip boots are almost always needed if the trapline is followed in marshy areas, streams, and shorelines. The boots can be left at home when cold weather puts a heavy layer of ice over the water. If the trapper walks the line he should carry a gunny sack to carry extra traps and bait on the way out, and the catch on the way back. If he has several miles of line he would be better off with a knapsack or a pack basket.

Muskrat trapping involves a lot of reaching into cold water. A pair of 31-inch rubber gloves or shoulder gauntlets will keep the hands and arms dry. A hatchet is necessary to cut stakes and to chop holes in a frozen pond. A chisel is a big help to cut holes in frozen ground or ice. A hand trowel is also useful before freeze-up. Wire is needed to prepare drown sets and to make tiedowns to drags and trees. Sidecutter pliers are needed for the wire. A few plastic bags carried in the pack will keep the water-soaked rats from getting the pack and its contents wet.

Bait and lures to make a variety of sets should be carried. In many stream and marsh areas, stake material is not available. Prepare a few stakes ahead of time and carry them in the pack. Cut a rubber band from a tire tube to hold the stakes together.

The No. 1 longspring is a good muskrat trap for drown sets. The No. 1 stop-loss can be used in sets where there is a possibility of a wring-off. Carry a few No. 1½ longspring traps or jump traps to use at sets that may take a fox or a coon. The 110 Conibear does a fine job in rat runways and in shallow water. Use them also in any other set except the feed-bed set. The baited repeat box trap in many open water areas works well.

Most muskrat traps are staked, whether on land or in the water. A wooden stake about 20 inches long and 1 inch square will do the job. The stakes can be cut with a table saw if one is available. This is a good stake for marshes or muddy streams. A willow stake made from a limb with a small branch section several inches long left 3 inches from the top is a good anchor. Check to see that the stake is set solid and that the trap ring cannot come over the top. If there is any doubt, wire the trap. Have the stake out in the water and below the surface. A caught rat will usually drown in 10 or more inches of water.

If the trapping is done in tidewater marshes where the water

Many young trappers start on muskrat. This boy holds a rat
taken from an Arizona canal. *(Photo: Norm Woolsey)*

level may rise a foot or more each day, use stakes that are 3 or 4 feet
long. About a foot above the bottom, leave a branch section protruding 2 or 3 inches. The trap ring will catch on this when the
stake is pulled and the trap will come up with the stake. If native
tree shoots are used as staking material, cut the stake at an angle so
that the light wood will make the trap easier to locate.

Traps set in air holes or near rat houses on a frozen lake or
marsh can be fastened to a small branch as a drag. The rat will
head for deep water and will drown. The branch will prevent the
chain end from going through the hole in the ice.

If the trapper works an area where he has exclusive trapping
rights and trap theft is not a problem, fluorescent paint or sur-
veyor's ribbon can be used to mark trap locations. Old-time trappers seem to have the ability to make more than a hundred sets,
though, and remember the location of every one.

The beginning trapper will find that the wring-off is his
biggest problem. If the muskrat is not quickly drowned, or caught
in a killer-type trap, it will likely twist off the caught foot and
escape. Many of these cripples make it back to the den, where they

die. Set the traps right and these losses will be minimized. The caught rat will be offered a quick and painless death.

SETS FOR MUSKRAT

Your scouting forays should have provided you with a number of potential hotspots for muskrat sets. The banks of streams, lakes, and marshes should offer the opportunity for hole sets. Slides that lead from the water to dry land are good bets for slide sets. Feed beds and feeder streams offer other possibilities. The muskrat is not difficult to trap if the trapper knows the animal and its habits.

Pocket Set

Dig a hole 5 inches in diameter and 16 inches deep into the edge of a steep or vertical bank. Slant the hole at about a 45-degree angle upward. Put the bottom of the hole slightly below the water level. Bait the hole with a carrot or an apple. Add lure by using a pencil-sized stick to serve as a lure stick. The lure will stay on the stick better if the upper end of the stick is mashed or slit with the knife. Dip this end of the stick in the lure and place the opposite end about 8 inches back from the hole entrance. Ram it into the mud. Leave about 1 inch of the stick above the mud. Set a No. 1 trap so that it is just inside the hole. Dig the trap in slightly so that it will be better hidden. Cover the pan and jaws with moss or waterlogged leaves. Stake the trap chain beneath the water. A 1-pound weight fastened to the chain will make this a drown set. If the water is shallow for several feet out, use a trap-chain extension long enough to let the rat make it to deeper water. A drowning wire fastened in deep water and at the shore edge with a slide lock, as used for beaver, will also work. A Conibear 110 can be substituted for the longspring with good results.

Natural-Hole Set

The muskrat will dig many holes along the water edge in the course of a year, and by trapping season many of these will be slightly above water level. Treat these holes the same as the pocket set. Bait and lure should be used. A simple lure can be made from the glands of the muskrat. The hole may also be visited by an occasional mink, so the trapper should make a well-staked set.

Slide Set

Set a No. 1 longspring trap in the water where the slide and water meet. Use a stop-loss trap if the water is shallow here and a drown set is difficult to prepare. Many times a Conibear 110 can be substituted. Stake the traps as far to the side of the slide as possible. The slide is probably used by more than one rat, and unless the killer trap is used, the caught rat will likely dig up the slide and ruin a good set location.

Feed-Bed Set

Muskrat have regular areas where they feed. Look for low mounds where they sit and munch on their favorite shoots. The trails leading to the feed beds are good locations for traps. So are the mounds, and so are the areas where they harvest the food.

Set the trap in about 2 inches of water, and stake the chain in deeper water. It is usually difficult to use a killer trap here. If one is used, it should be baited with a carrot, an apple, or a piece of the feed material located there. Fasten the bait to the trigger of the Conibear. Bend the trigger prongs to the center to make a base for the bait. Some trappers prefer having the trigger prongs pointing up with the bait partially in the water.

Den-Hole Set

The main rat den can be located by watching for a patch of dirty water. Usually there is a large mound of dirt at the entrance. It may be marked by a smooth area where all of the mud and loose material have been tamped and polished by the muskrat traffic.

These holes usually produce several rats. Set the No. 1 longspring or the Conibear here. If the longspring is used, put the jaws just inside the hole. If the Conibear is used, set it far enough out so that the closing jaws will not jam on the face of the hole. Stake the longspring into deeper water to make it a drown set.

Lodge Set

Many states do not permit trapping within a designated distance of a lodge. This is an important protection for the rat, as it gives it a sanctuary to live and reproduce. If a rat lodge is damaged or destroyed, many of the muskrat die before they can locate another safe area.

If the lodge is trapped, set No. 1 traps on the paths leading up onto the sides of the lodge. Make all sets drown sets. A caught rat that is not drowned will create such a disturbance around the lodge that damage might be done. In frozen areas where only the lodge is visible, the trapper can dig a hole at the longer edges of the lodge until a runway to the center chamber is found. Stake a trap into the passageway, in water that is as deep as you can reach.

Put the trap in the shallow water close to the chamber. A 110 Conibear can many times be used. If lodge trapping is practiced, make an estimate of the number of muskrat in the colony. This can be done by considering the size of the lodge and the amount of feeding activity nearby. Take only a safe number of rats before pulling the traps. Plug the hole before leaving so that the remaining rats will have a safe place to spend the rest of the winter. The rats left will repopulate the lodge when summer comes. The trapper will actually be money ahead to stay away from the lodges. He can take his muskrat from the surrounding area without molesting the rat in its winter home.

Stream Set

Many times a stream chokes up with weeds, brush, or rocks and the muskrat must travel through a narrow passage. Some smaller streams have areas that can be constructed to force the rat through a narrow opening. Prepared passageways should be finished several weeks before the season to give the rats a chance to become accustomed to this new feature.

Use a No. 1 longspring here if the water is deep enough to make a drown set. Otherwise use the No. 1 stop-loss or the Conibear. These sets will also take mink. A mink caught in a trap set for rat is a bonus that will leave the trapper in good humor for the rest of the day.

Toilet-Post Set

Many times muskrat use special areas to deposit their waste. These may consist of raised areas in the water, rocks, log ends, or cattail clumps. The toilet is often used by every muskrat that comes by.

Set the trap at the edge of the rock, raised sod, or cattail clump. The water is usually shallow here, so a drowning wire must be used. A stick with muskrat lure helps to bring the rats in. Jam the stick in the water with the lure end protruding just forward of the trap.

Log-End Set

This set can be fixed as a toilet set or as a baited Conibear set. The log being used as a toilet stop should have a flat spot chopped out just under the water level. If the log is in calm water with no tidal change, set the No. 1 trap in the flattened section. Wire or staple the trap chain to the underside of the log. Pick the side that has the deepest water. Put a light layer of water weeds over the trap. Pick up a few of the droppings and put them on the log a few inches above the trap.

A log end also makes a good Conibear set. Chop the top of the log to make it flat from the water edge out for about 6 inches. Another way is to chop a groove in the log about an inch deep and across the log at the water's edge. This allows a 6-inch section of limb to be nailed solidly to the log to hold the trap in place. Use a limb that is an inch or so in diameter. Staple or wire the trap chain to the side or bottom of the log in deep water. With the spring pulled down, the trigger will be up and the free jaws tight against the nailed limb section. Spread the trigger wires slightly.

A baited Conibear can be used here. Bend the trigger wires in and fasten a cattail section, an apple, or a carrot between the trigger wires. The trap will be easily seen by hunters and fishermen, however, and might disappear. Once the catch is made the trap and the trapped fall into the water and are concealed.

Ceramic-Tile Set

Marshes and swamps are often drained with ceramic tile. These offer excellent set locations. Below the tile there are often small streams that run year-round, and the rats use the tile openings as travelways. Use the Conibear 110 or the No. 1 longspring staked for drowning.

Feeder-Stream Set

Small streams that enter a marsh or a larger stream are travel routes for the muskrat. The streams offer a safe and easy passageway. If the stream is shallow and only a few inches wide the Conibear trap can be used with good results. A No. 1 stop-loss will also do the job. On larger streams use a controlled-travel-route set. A pocket set with lure or bait will also take rats.

Pushup and Air-Hole Sets

Much muskrat country has marshes that are frozen during the winter months. The muskrat live and work under the ice and have small mud and wadding mounds that rise a few inches above the ice. These will be noticed out to 100 yards away from the lodge. The rats use these structures to get air; the larger ones are also used as feed stations. The mounds are most often located among the weeds and cattails. Mark these locations with a stick or by tying reeds or cattails together. Use string, cloth, a branch, or any other item to mark them. When the snow falls the locations are otherwise hard to find.

Cut into the pushup. Stake a No. 1 longspring so that the rat can get back under the ice and drown. Remove a double handful of mud and feeder material and put it aside to reseal the hole made for the trap. The hole must be covered or the water there will soon freeze solid. A big lodge may have a dozen or more of these pushups.

Cut-Ins for Bank Sets

When most of the rats in a small pond or marsh are using bank dens, the trapper should mark the hole locations at the point they enter the water. For winter trapping, push a 3-to-4-foot willow stake into the ground next to the passageway. When snow covers the ground you can dig or chop your way down to the den and make the set. Otherwise you will not be able to locate them after a snowstorm.

If the den hole is narrow, enlarge it to about 8 by 10 inches at the entrance. This will be under water. Stake a No. 1 trap so that the caught rat will stay in the enlarged area and will drown. Leave enough room so that other rats are able to pass, and use the dirt and mud removed to seal the hole that has been cut in. If a board is handy, use it to cover the sealed hole and then cover the board with snow. Do not remove the marker stake. If prepared properly the set will take a number of rats.

CHECKING TRAPS

In most areas the muskrat line should be checked daily. The trapper will collect more rats and if the rat does not drown, daily checking will help to control wring-offs. Too, the caught rat that is dead and visible from the bank may be mutilated or stolen by predators.

Check every trap. The drowners may have a well-hidden caught rat. Open all cut-ins, runways, and pushups and feel for plugged runways, sprung traps, or your catch.

Some sets may need readjusting when a caught animal has damaged the set. Add fresh bait or lure as needed. If the runway sets don't produce in a few days, pull the traps and put them at a more productive site. Replug the opening and leave an air hole about an inch across. Observe the air hole as you pass when checking the trapline to see if it has been plugged. If so, a rat has moved into the area and the trap can be reset.

When the rat is taken from the trap, shake the excess water from the fur. Put it in a small plastic bag if it is to be carried in the pack. This will keep the other pack contents dry.

Some trappers have day jobs and run their lines after dark. If you are traveling a long line, an electric head lamp is a good investment, to keep both hands free while running the line. Carry extra batteries and bulbs. A walk through the marsh without a light is an experience no trapper wants to repeat.

SKINNING

Muskrat are easy to skin; the job can be done in a minute or two. Use a stick or the handle of a hammer to break off the four large front teeth. This makes skinning the mouth easier. Lay the rat on its back and grab the near hind foot with the left hand. Cut in a straight line from the base of the heel to the base of the tail. Continue around the tail base and on to the base of the opposite heel. Pull the hide free at the back of the tail. Cut the hide free, leaving about an inch of the leathery skin of the tail on the hide. Pull the skin loose from the stomach and pull each hind leg free from the hide. Hold the back end of the rat with the right hand and the pelt with the left (assuming you're right-handed). Pull the hide loose to the front legs. Grasp the front-leg fur with the left hand and the fore leg with the right. Give a fast pull and the fur will tear off at the wrists. Another pull brings the hide free to the ears. Cut the ears free from the skull and pull the hide down over the eyes, lips, and nose.

If the fur is wet, strip away any extra water and turn the pelt fur side out to let the fur dry. Always have the fur side out when it is being transported along the line. The pelt should be hung to dry when home or camp is reached. If a large number need drying, you might invest in a forced-air fan.

STRETCHING

When the fur is dry, put the skin on a solid drying board with the fur to the inside. Remove all fat and any flesh. Do not try to remove the thin flesh layer that covers the rat's back.

If many fat rats are caught, the trapper can use the wringer from an old-fashioned washing machine to squeeze the fat from the hide. Two people are needed for this operation.

A clean pelt should be pulled onto the stretcher until it is tight. Use three nails to secure the back in place. Do the same to the stomach. On the stomach side put one nail at center and one in each of the rear legs. Hang or stand in a cool, dry, well-ventilated area until totally dry. Oil within the skin tissue should not be removed, only excess fat.

The commercial wire frames work well if a large number of rats are to be handled. Many trappers make their own wood stretchers, using ¼- or ⅜-inch stock. Make three sizes: small, medium, and large; the most-used will be the medium. The board should have a tapered point, and 5 inches below the point the board should measure 5 inches wide. The base measurement should be 7 inches. The board length is 22 inches. Make the small stretcher board ¾ inch smaller at the shoulders and 1 inch smaller at the base. The large board should measure 6 inches at the shoulders and 7½ inches at the base.

When the pelts are dry they can be taken from the stretchers and stacked. Keep them in a cool, dry place. Protect the pelts from household pets. Even well-fed cats and dogs will often eat the dried pelts.

15
Beaver

The beaver is the largest rodent of North America. The adult averages 25 to 30 inches in length with another 10 inches of tail. The tail, of course, is not furred. Body weight varies from 30 to 60 pounds; beaver have been taken that have weighed more than 100 pounds. The "blanket beaver," as established by the Hudson Bay Fur Company, must exceed 50 pounds. Beaver kits weigh from 8 to 16 pounds.

The body of the beaver is heavy-set and compact. The front legs are small. The rear legs are much larger and the feet are webbed. The hairless tail is flat and covered with large scales. Beaver color ranges from nearly black to a golden brown. Much of the color variation follows distinct geographic patterns.

The beaver is aquatic and is seldom found any great distance from water. It leaves the water to feed but will return to it to live. It may leave the water to seek out a new territory and then be seen miles from any stream, but it is just exploring, and will not ordinarily be found in such a situation. Look for the beaver near lake shores, rivers, and streams. Although once fairly common through all of North America the beaver disappeared from much of its former range due to early overtrapping. It is now found in most of its original habitat, thanks to transplanting and better management.

The beaver needs fairly deep water to exist. If it lives in natural or artificial impoundments, it is a bank beaver and exists without any dam-building activity. In areas of shallow streams and rivers the beaver will create deeper water by building a dam made of mud, sticks, and other debris.

Breeding takes place during the winter, and about four young are born three months later. The young stay with the parents for the first year and may stay in the family unit until their third year. Then they often strike out on their own to establish new territory.

This bank beaver has a burrow under the brush at right top. *(Photo: Gerry Blair)*

Every beaver in the colony is a worker. They participate in dam building, lodge building, and bringing in the winter's food supply. The young beaver do their share of the work close to home, and the older beaver venture farther out. They work mainly at night. The work period starts at dusk and will continue until shortly after dawn.

Beaver live mainly on the bark and tender inner layer of trees such as willow, birch, aspen, and cottonwood. They also eat the buds from these trees and some grass and roots during the summer; the bark and branches are the winter food. The beaver will stockpile large amounts of log sections and branches in the deeper water close to the lodge for winter feeding.

In the northern habitat, the beaver spends the winter under ice. The lodge has one or two entrances. When ice covers the water surface, the beaver spends more time in the lodge, for the construction of the dam has been completed and the cutting and moving of winter food to the stockpile is finished. The lodge had its final maintenance and inspection just before the final freeze-up. The lodge will have a few small air holes left at its peak, and the peak is protected by large pole sections imbedded in mud and frozen solid during winter months. During the winter, beaver cut short sections from their green-wood stockpile and may feed on it underwater or return to the lodge with it. Most branch sections are removed and left just outside the lodge and under the ice. The dam is inspected during the winter and any maintenance needed is carried out. A constant water level is kept if at all possible. Adult beaver may check smaller dams of the area by going over the dam and traveling under ice. If the ice thickens until their food supply is frozen the beaver die.

HARMFUL AND BENEFICIAL EFFECTS
Overpopulation of beaver can cause problems to both farmers and fruit growers. The dam-building activity sometimes causes flooding of fields and crop damage. Beaver will chew down fruit and shade trees and sometimes dam irrigation ditches, causing extra work for the farmer. If not harvested they overproduce and damage the habitat by cutting down all trees in the area.

The beaver is, however, an ally of man in water conservation and erosion control. In centuries past, the beaver's dam construction and tree removal turned much of the country into the inviting meadowland that was the first settled by the pioneers. Beaver dams also provide good habitat for fish, waterfowl, and other less talented water lovers such as the otter, the mink, and the muskrat.

VALUE AS A FURBEARER
Beaver pelt prices, like other fur prices, fluctuate with the current market demands. In the first half of the 1800s, prime beaver plews (pelts) might bring the trapper as much as $8, a fantastic price when many men worked in those days for $2 or $3 a week. A change in fashion caused the pelts to go to almost nothing, and few were trapped. Then the prices came back, as they always do. A good beaver pelt would bring the trapper $100 about the time that the Great Depression began. As of this writing the pelt brings an average of about $14. In Canada, during the winter of '69-'70, almost 500,000 beaver pelts were collected.

Other parts of the beaver have some value as a cash crop. The castors and oil glands are used as a base for many perfumes and as an ingredient in many trapping scents.

TRAPS FOR BEAVER

Nothing smaller than a No. 3 trap should be used for taking beaver. If the Conibear is used, the 330 will do a good job. The No. 4 longspring or underspring is also a good choice. The No. 4½, 14, 48, and 114 Newhouse are still used by some trappers. They are heavy if the trapper must pack them any distance. Snares can also be used to take beaver, particularly in areas where the big rodents have trails through heavy grass or brush. The snares are light and are less expensive.

As with other traps, check all beaver traps during the off season. Check the working condition and strength. Make any modifications. Derust, color, and wax the traps, not so much for the beaver's benefit but to keep the traps from rusting and to keep them working smoothly. A drowning slide should be on every trap chain to fit the trap for deep water use.

BEAVER SIGN

If the trapper is new to the area and plans on trapping there for several seasons, he should scout the area thoroughly and get an estimate of the beaver population. Beaver sign is mostly in the form of dams, gnawed trees, beaver runways along the water's edge, tracks in the mud, and, most important, lodges. The trapper may see swimming animals at dusk and dawn or hear the sound of their flat tails slapping the water.

You should check for the number of dams and lodges. Determine if the dams are new or are several years old. Work the river and lake banks to find the feeding areas.

When a trapper has worked an area for a year or two he will know where the main colonies are located. He should take a good percent of the large and extra-large beaver and leave the kits. He will then have a beaver population to trap on a continuing basis.

The beaver's track is distinctive. The small front foot and the large hind foot are a dead giveaway. The hind foot of a grown beaver will leave a track that is about 6 inches long and half that wide. The front foot will be about 2½ by 1½ inches. When walking, they usually cover the front print with the rear foot. The stride varies from 4 to 8 inches depending on the animal's size.

Beaver ponds that have been heavily silted may have no beaver population or may have a loner or outcast. The same areas may show increased beaver activity the following year. The trapper should keep good records as to number, sex, and age of beaver taken from each area, and the type of set. The recordkeeping will pay off when the trapper starts a new season and wants to determine the best location for his sets.

When a feeding area is found, the trapper should make note of the distance between the cut on the trees and the ground. A big beaver will cut higher than a kit or yearling, and the trapper will know he has some adults in the area. As mentioned earlier, the older beaver are the ones that work the greatest distance from the main dam and lodge.

SPECIAL EQUIPMENT

Harvesting of beaver is a specialized phase of trapping and requires some specialized equipment. On lakes and large rivers you will need some type of boat. A light 12-foot flat-bottom pushed by a 10-horse engine will do a good job. Carry oars in case the motor gets cranky. A good pair of hip boots are a must. Ten-inch sidecutters, a hatchet, extra wire, sliders, and extra traps are needed. When larger Newhouse traps are used, be sure to carry a 10-inch crescent wrench to take a trap apart in case you catch fingers or hand and can't get to the trap with your feet. Have several metal U clips with adjusted holes for a cotter pin to use on a set 220 and 330 Conibear. These are important safety devices. Don't forget a container of waterproof matches, a set of rain gear, and a good sharp skinning knife. Keep the equipment where it is easy to reach. Check the equipment box daily before setting out on the line. The beaver line should be run as soon after daylight as possible. This will minimize losses.

Put extra wire in the pack to use in drown sets. Heavy telephone wire from abandoned lines works well. Metal and rock weights should be prepared and positioned before the start of the season. They should weigh at least 30 pounds. If the weight is positioned next to the trap a lighter weight can be used, and a 10-pounder may do the job if the water is deep.

The pole-ring set uses a slender pole that is weighted on one end and fastened or staked at the other end. Leave a few short limb

This log leading to the beaver dam would be an excellent walkway for many animals. *(Photo: Bill Musgrove)*

sections on the pole. They should be small enough so a chain ring will slide over them on the way down but will catch on the way back up. A few nails pounded in at an angle will serve the same purpose. A beaver that takes the trap into deep water will soon drown. If the trapper knows trap locations prior to trapping season he can construct these sets before the season and set the trap when the season opens.

The pole can also be fastened at both ends, one end placed solidly into the muddy bottom and then staked at the top. Fasten the trap with 6 to 8 feet of extra chain at the base. The beaver makes its way to deep water, winds up on the pole, and drowns.

A long slender pole 8 to 20 feet long can be used to make a drowner. Sharpen one end and force it into the bottom of the dam or river and in deep water. Drive a stake by the water's edge and secure the small end of the pole. The trap-chain ring slides on the pole and allows the beaver to get to deep water and drown. Use about 4 to 8 feet of trap chain for this set. Leave many 3-

to-4-inch-long branch stubs at the deep-water end for the beaver to wind chain on and drown.

SETS FOR BEAVER

There are a number of sets you can use for beaver. The better ones ensure that the animal drowns before it can wring off.

Bank-Slide Set

A beaver often leaves and enters the water at constant locations and creates a condition called a slide. This is an excellent location for a trap. Put the trap in front of the slide in 8 to 10 inches of water. The beaver leaves and enters the water with its front feet held back or by its side. Unless the trap is positioned for a rear-foot catch, the beaver will likely spring the trap with its throat or chest and will escape.

Fasten a 10- or 12-pound weight about 8 inches back on the trap chain. The trap chain should be at least 6 feet long. When the trap springs the beaver's first thought is to find the safety of deep water. The weight will go with it and will prevent it from surfacing for air. The end of the trap chain should be staked at the water's edge or wired to a tree or tree root.

The water should be at least 3 feet deep for a good drown set. If the shore water stays shallow for some distance, use a heavy weight of 30 to 50 pounds. This can be a rock, a piece of metal, or a sack of sand or gravel. Fasten the wire with the drowning slide on the wire. Fasten the free end of the wire to a stake or tiedown on the shore. The drowning wire can be made long enough to get the beaver out to deep water. The end of the wire with the weight is placed in the deep water and the other end is attached to shore. The one-way slide lets the beaver follow the wire to deep water and prevents its return. The trapper can collect the beaver by pulling in the drowning wire. If the drowning wire is used in a river, the weighted end should be placed at a slight angle downstream.

Underwater Bait Set

Use a section of a food tree and secure it in the lake bottom in about 20 inches of water. Leave a few inches of the top above water. Put two traps with the jaws parallel to the probable approach route. Tie the traps to a heavy drowning weight or the drowning wire and slide-lock setup. The beaver will stand on its hind legs to get to the bait stick and will be caught.

Scent Set

Travel routes are good bets for a scent set. If the set is in shallow water the beaver will walk up rather than swim. Traps should be placed 4 to 6 inches back of the scent. Dig the traps in so they will not flop over if a jaw is stepped on. The drowning wire with slip lock can be used with this set most of the time. A good scent can be made by grinding together dried beaver castor and oil gland. A little amount goes a long way. Use only a drop or two if in liquid form. If it is a paste, use a drop about the size of a pencil head. Other furbearers often come to beaver scent and are caught.

Dam-Runway Set

The beaver have water runways over their dams to use when moving from dam to dam. Set the trap on the upper side of the runway in about 10 inches of water. Dig the trap in slightly and position the jaws parallel with the water flow. Use a drowning wire and slide lock or a 10-foot chain with a weight attached near the trap end. Do not destroy or damage the dam; to do so demonstrates a lack of interest in the wildlife of the area and no concern for the next year's trapping.

The Conibear 330 is efficient at taking the beaver as it goes over the dam. Make the set so that the beaver, or otter if one comes by, is encouraged to go through the trap. Set the trigger wires in a V pattern for best results. Anchor the trap securely to the upper side of the dam.

Shore-Trail Set

A beaver can be trapped when it uses its dry-land trails but will often wring off before the trapper comes to collect. The Conibear 220 or 330 is a better bet here. Do not use the Conibear if nontarget animals are likely to be caught. Set the trap so that the jaws strike across the top and bottom of the body, not against the side. Fasten the trap chain to a heavy drag or have it well staked. Most large beaver will fight the trap until their last breath. Beaver taken on dry land will spoil rapidly unless the day weather stays cold, and predators may eat them. Check the traps as early in the day as possible.

Water-Runway Set

When a 3- or 4-foot-deep channel runs between dams or waterways the beaver will use it as a water trail. Make a picket-pole structure to force the beaver to go through a controlled center opening. Leave about 12 inches between the center vertical poles.

Put 2-inch-diameter crossbars between these poles. Leave an opening at the bottom a foot square. Place longspring or under-spring jump traps on each side of the opening. Tie down to the second stake from the center and reinforce the tiedown.

If a Conibear is used, add a bottom crossbar slipped through the springs and the next upper crossbar between the upper jaws. This keeps the trap stable and in good position. This set will also take otter. It works in open or iced water.

Under-Ice Bait Set

Beaver trapping is somewhat restricted when cold weather comes and ice forms on the water, but if the trapper knows where the beaver feed under ice he can still take beaver. Wait until the ice gets thick enough to support your weight. Use a single-bitted ax and an ice chisel to cut a hole with a 12-inch diameter. Drive a dry wooden pole into the lake bottom until it is solid. Use a pole that will fit through the spring rings, and wire the trap chain and spring rings to secure the trap. A bait of fresh aspen or birch is then wired to the stake that will fit between the jaws. The trap, chain, and bait should be set and secured before the pole is positioned. For extra safety in securing the traps, wire a 3-foot crosspiece on the pole where it sticks above the ice. This will prevent the beaver from making away with the setup if he is able to pull the stake from the lake bottom. The water depth here, of course, must be fairly shallow; 1 to 4 feet deep is about right. Finish off the set by pushing snow into the chopped hole, cover with a few evergreen branches, and pile on more snow until level. This keeps the hole from freezing so solidly and makes it much easier to rechop it to check the traps.

Removing a caught beaver from an ice set can be a problem. Some ice will have reformed on the hole, and this must be removed. In very cold weather the beaver carcass may have frozen solid to the ice. Chop and chisel the beaver free, taking extra ice out with the beaver. Do not try to pull the beaver free of the ice or the pelt will be damaged. Cutting too close to the beaver fur will also cause damage. Do not pull chunks of ice off the fur. Strike the ice with the flat side of the ax and the ice will shatter and drop off.

SNARES

Snares are small, light, and inexpensive and are easy to set up. They are difficult for the trap thief to see. The trapper will find that snares become easy to use as he gains experience. In some locations the snare will do as good a job as either a Conibear or a leghold trap.

The loop of the snare should be 8 to 10 inches in diameter to take a beaver. Center the loop over a runway, a hole, a trail, or a controlled channel. The No. 2 coyote snare will do a good job on beaver.

Water Snare

Water snares should be set so that about 3 inches of the loop are below water. This will result in mostly neck catches. Snares placed in beaver holes below the water are centered and several inches up from the bottom. A beaver leaves an underwater hole swimming close to the bottom with the front feet pulled in close to the body. Snares must be securely fastened. A big beaver will work up a lot of pull, and the snare must not come loose.

Land Snare

Land snares are set where beaver work feeding areas or travel short distances overland. Anchor the snares securely to a stout tiedown. Position the snare so that the bottom of the loop is 4 to 6 inches off the ground. Use an 8 to 10-inch loop. Use small twigs to secure the snare loop and make the loop the logical passageway. Use common sense when setting the snare. Like the Conibear trap, snares are nonselective. A snare big enough to take a beaver will quickly kill a dog and injure domestic stock. Do not use near residences or in any area where men commonly hunt dogs. If in cattle or sheep country, remember that both of these enterprises involve the use of dogs.

When a catch is made at a dry-land snare location it is usually best to move the snare to a new place for resetting. The animal will tear up the set as it struggles to get free. It is usually quicker to find a new location than to rebuild the old set.

PACKING

Many beaver trappers attend traplines in part or totally by walking. With the weight of an adult, after the first catch the trapper is loaded. This leaves two choices: skin the beaver or haul them. An experienced beaver skinner will clean-skin, while most trappers rough-skin and flesh later. A single beaver can be packed. With a good cover of snow, two or more beaver are easily pulled on a short toboggan or a snow saucer. The snow saucer should be at least 3 feet in diameter with turned-up edges and equipped with pulling ropes on one side.

SKINNING

The beaver is more difficult to skin than most other furbearers. To do the job right, and do it fast, takes practice and a good technique. A sharp knife is a must. There is more than one way to skin a beaver. Many trappers have their own systems.

Lay the beaver on a table that is a comfortable working height. Cut the fur loose from around the base of the tail. This will be the area where the fur ends and the scales begin. Cut the fur loose from all four feet at the wrists. You may want to cut the feet completely off at the wrists and get them out of the way. The tail can also be cut off where the fur ends and discarded. If a chopping block is handy, a hatchet can be used to take off the feet and tail quickly.

Split the pelt from the underside of the lip in a straight line to the base of the tail on the belly side of the beaver. Skin the fur away from the body on one side of the slit, working from the chin to the tail. If the beaver is placed in a skinning trough, stomach up, so that the hide can be pulled down over one side, longer cuts can be made. Skin the animal clean as you go and it will save work later on. The skin is thin around the legs and extra care is needed to prevent cutting or tearing. Pull the hide over the leg stumps, and do not split the hide. Cut the ears free from the skull and skin out the eyes, lips, and nose.

A skinning trough can be prepared in back country by using two 4-foot poles, one 6 inches and one 8 inches in diameter. These should be 4 inches apart and nailed or notched into a log at both ends. Have the larger pole knot- and bark-free and use it to pull the hide over when skinning.

FLESHING, CLEANING, AND CASTOR REMOVAL

The beaver must be fleshed before it is stretched to dry unless it was clean-skinned. Use a fleshing beam made of smooth knot-free wood. If pine or fir is used check to see that there are no pitch pockets. Put the pelt skin side up on the beam and nail the head area in place. Work the flesher from the head to the tail, removing all flesh and fat. A few trips to the fleshing board will make any trapper a clean skinner in the future.

The pelt should be cleaned of all dirt, pitch, and fat. Use

kerosene to dissolve the pitch. If kerosene is used, the pelt should be washed in warm water and a mild detergent to take out the kerosene and remove any fat or oil left from fleshing. If the pelt is bloody it should be first washed in cold water to remove the blood.

The castors are located forward and on each side of the anal opening. Cut the castors loose and remove excess tissue. Do not break into the glandular sac. If the castors are correctly removed and dried they will bring extra money when payday comes.

STRETCHING

The beaver pelt can be stretched round or slightly oval. Do not overstretch. The standard method to find the correct width of the pelt is to tack the nose to the drying board. The length of the skin, minus 1 inch per foot of length, will provide the correct diameter of the circle. If you raise the tail section slightly, the hide can be stretched exactly round. Some trappers make the width identical to the unstretched length. This provides a larger pelt but it also thins the hide, and the fur buyer may not be fooled.

To stretch oval, tack the nose of the hide and the bottom of the hide to the stretching board. The width of the hide should be two-thirds of its unstretched length. Tack the hide to the board in an oval shape. In the past, the round was the standard method of handling beaver. In recent years many trappers are going to the oval stretch. Check the local fur buyer to find the stretch that he prefers.

If the drying board is solid, use small shingle nails to fasten the hide to the stretcher. Nail the hide every ½ inch. The fur goes to the inside. Make three sizes of beaver boards: 30-inch square, 40-inch square, and 50-inch square. Use ¾-inch plywood and both sides can be used to stretch a hide. Some trappers just saw a 4 x 8-foot plywood sheet into two pieces. The 4-foot-square pieces can be used to stretch most hides. If many beaver are being handled you may want to cut a hole in the middle of the board to allow air to hit the pelt from both sides. Cut a circle with an 18-inch diameter from the center of the board.

Beaver hides can also be tacked to building walls or doors. Wherever the pelt is stretched, all holes in the hide must be sewed. The leg skins are pulled out and the extra skin trimmed. The four holes from the feet are closed by using six or eight nails on a drying board or by sewing.

William Ross, an eastern Oregon trapper, displays a well-handled beaver skin.
(Photo: Bill Musgrove)

Hoop Stretching

A beaver hoop can be made from slender saplings. Most are made
from willow; wild cherry also works well. Many trappers use
hardwood strips, and some use metal hoops.

In lacing, pick a hoop that is slightly larger than the length of the hide. Fasten the nose, sides, and tail area in position. Use a large curved needle or stitching awl to lace the hide to the frame. Lace loosely the first time around, making the stitches about an inch apart. Now go around the pelt a second time, tightening the laces, until the hide assumes the desired shape. Most hoop-stretched pelts are finished round.

When the pelt is dry, remove it from the stretcher and store it. Pelts can be stacked atop each other fur to fur. Keep the storage room cool and well ventilated. The dried skins can be rolled if necessary but should never be folded.

COOKING BEAVER
Beaver is used as food by many trappers. The skinned tail, with the fat trimmed off, has a good flavor when boiled with a pot of dried beans. The hams and the small of the back are lighter and very tasty when roasted. Beaver can also be cooked by boiling for soup or stew or ground as hamburger (beaverburger?). Beaver meat makes good dog food and chicken feed, and a good bait to take any of the flesh eaters.

16
Mink

The mink is probably the best-known member of the weasel family. It has been trapped and raised commercially for its fur since before the Civil War. The mink is a small animal, weighing from 1 to 4 pounds. The 2-foot-long body is slender, and the legs are short. The tail may total a third of the body length. The neck is short and the head small. The fur is usually a rich chocolate brown with a white chin patch. The amount of white under the chin varies; it sometimes extends all the way back to the stomach. The female mink is about half the weight of the male.

Breeding takes place in early spring (March and April). After a gestation period of forty to seventy-six days the young are born. The litter ranges from four to ten kits. The den may be located in a large brush pile, an abandoned beaver lodge, or an old muskrat burrow.

The mink is found throughout the United States and Canada. It is seldom found in the Southwest, perhaps because of the lack of riparian habitat, but is common in most other parts of North America. The mink is at home on either land or water but is more commonly found close to rivers and marshes. The diet is variable. The young leave the den in the fall to locate their own hunting areas. Some are nomadic as adults and will travel long distances overland, or up and down riverbanks. The home territory varies with the amount of food available and the time of the year. The male travels a lot during the mating season. The female stays in her home territory and lets the male come to her. If the female's den and foraging areas are not bothered there will be a steady supply of male mink coming to the territory, and a crop of young raised year after year.

Fish is a common food for the mink. The mink catches the fish alive by outswimming them underwater. Mink will also eat mice, frogs, birds, muskrat, and other small animals. Although small,

The mink has been crossbred in captivity to produce a wide variety of fur color. This violet strain is one of the most popular. Like other members of the weasel family the mink is vicious and unfriendly. *(Photo: U.S. Dept. of Agriculture)*

they are vicious fighters and will sometimes tackle and kill an animal that is much larger than they are.

HARMFUL EFFECTS

The mink has a taste for fresh muskrat, and this will often get it into trouble with the fur trapper. One large male mink was known to have cleaned out the rats from seven large rat houses in a 10-acre cattail marsh. Mink also take some waterfowl. Adult birds are not often bothered unless they have been injured or are sick. Mink occasionally get into the henhouse. They also will eat rabbits and domestic ducks if they get a chance. If a mink is causing problems with domestic animals, it would be best to live-trap the culprit and move it into an area away from the ranch house.

VALUE AS A FURBEARER

Mink have always been a much-sought furbearer. Mink pelts have remained at a stable value longer than most other fur. The fur is handsome and it wears well.

Although the industry of raising mink for its fur is large, wild fur is still in great demand. It is an animal that can respond well to trapping pressure.

Mink are prime during early November in the Northern states and Canada. The higher elevations of the western United States will also see a November priming. The fur will prime a bit later farther to the south. Do not trap the mink before the fur comes prime, otherwise the pelts will be poor and the fur buyer will not award top price.

MINK SIGN

A potential mink trapping area should be fully scouted prior to the start of trapping. Look for small droppings at brush piles and log jams, around beaver lodges, and at the edges of bridges, culvert ends, cut banks, and where slide rock may come down to streams or lakes. The droppings are 1 or 2 inches long and tapered at each end. They are as big around as a pencil. Mink, like other animals, will often set up regular scent-post locations.

If there are mink in the area their tracks will likely appear in soft mud along the banks of marshes, streams, and lakes. Dusty areas in trails near the water might also show tracks. If there is snow on the ground it will carry a history of the mink movement. The trapper will be able to find where the mink enters and leaves the water, its favorite brush piles, and the hunting activities away from the water. The mink tracks are about the size of a quarter, and more tapered than round. The walking track is about 2 inches apart; the short jump of a running mink will show 12 to 18 inches between paired imprints.

Mink will make many trips between the water and the land cover. After many trips a narrow trail is developed. These trails are a good place to trap.

A successful mink trapper will learn to recognize any mink sign that he comes across. He must develop a good knowledge of the mink, the habits of the animal, and the habitat in which it lives. If he is to be successful year after year he must not trap an area bare. Leave enough mink in the area to repopulate it for next year's trapping.

TRAPS FOR MINK

The best trap to use to take mink varies somewhat with the area and the climate. The No. 11 and the No. 1½ longspring and the No. 1½ underspring and coilspring will all take mink. A strong (new) No. 1 longspring will also take mink, and so will No. 2 jump traps. The killer traps in the small sizes will do the job also.

When possible, the trap should be set so that the animal will drown and be out of sight when caught. This will minimize trap theft and will also protect the mink from predators such as the great horned owl.

All traps should be in good condition. Also needed is a pair of strong sidecutters, extra wire in 8 or 10 gauge, a hatchet, rubber gloves, stakes and weights, and drags. If the trapping is done near the water, the trapper will find that a pair of hip boots opens a lot of new trapping territory to him.

SETS FOR MINK

A variety of land and water sets will take mink. They are a curious animal, and are mostly dumb. Human odor around the trap will not bother most mink. Once in a while, if a mink has had its toes pinched a few times, it will get trap-smart. It may live for years in the trapping area and tempt the trapper to spend a lot of time trying to collect it. This is a mistake. Concentrate on the uneducated mink. It will be easier to trap and will sell for just about as much as the smart one. It might be poor business to spend time on catching the trap-wise mink when the same amount of time might yield four or five dumb ones. Too, the trapper wants to leave some mink in the area for reproductive purposes. Might as well leave the smart one.

Bank-Hole Set

The bank-hole set is probably the best all-around taker of mink. The set can be dug either above or at the water level. If bait is used, the above-water set is preferred. The hole should be about 4 to 6 inches in diameter and nearly straight back into the bank for about 18 inches. The mink must leave the water about a foot to enter the baited hole. Many mink travel along the shore edge while hunting and so would come in direct contact with the hole. The carcass of a muskrat, a part of a fish, or a small bird will do for the bait. The bait should be fastened about 6 inches in past the trap. When checking the hole, or attempting to pull out the bait, the mink will get itself caught. The bait should be changed often to keep it fresh. Cover the trap with leaves or fine grass to give the set a natural appearance. A small amount of mink urine or scent by the hole will often bring the mink in to investigate.

If the water-level set is used it should be dug as above, with the mouth of the hole only half-filled with water. A drowning wire or a weighted drag should be attached to the trap. When drowned, the animal will be out of sight. This will also give it a chance to pull away from the set and not damage it. If the sets are prepared before trapping season, a rock can be wired and positioned to serve as a drag. Use a 2-to-4-pound rock and wire it close to the trap. Tie 4 feet of 8-gauge wire to the end of the trap chain and stake the free end below the hole in the water. When caught, the mink will head for deep water and drown rapidly.

If the set is made by a shallow stream and the drown set cannot be used, tie a grapple hook with about 4 feet of chain. The grapples are easily made and will not cost the trapper an arm and a leg in supplies. When the grapples are not in use on the mink line they can be used for coon or fox.

When a stream is running at a constant level, a hole can be dug horizontally in the bank. Dig the hole right at the water's edge with about 2 inches of water standing in the bottom of the hole. Make the hole big enough to let a mink in, about 6 inches in diameter. The trap will have about an inch of water over its top and will be hidden from the mink. Put a small amount of mink scent above the hole. This makes a simple drown set by staking the trap chain in deep water or by using an attached weight.

Blind Set

The blind set works very well for mink if the trapper can locate a trail. If the trap is set where the mink enter or leave the water, put the trap out in the water so that it is covered. Now cover the trap with moss or leaves, not for the mink's benefit, but to hide it from trap thieves. Traps set on dry land should have a pan cover and dirt (a light covering of leaves will also do the job) and should be staked or tied to a grapple or weight.

Log-End Set

A log that lies in the water at an angle makes a natural place for a mink to stop. Drill or chop a small hole on the upstream side above water level and put in a small amount of mink scent. Chop a flat

Mink will work the water's edge and will explore around the roots of every tree that borders the stream. *(Photo: Gerry Blair)*

spot out of the log just below the water level. It should be deep enough to accept the trap. Make the set as natural-appearing as possible. A small amount of bait can also be used with the set if desired. This set will also take raccoon and muskrat if there are any in the area.

Runway Set

A natural runway between a log, stump, rock, and the bank are good locations for a mink set. Use small rocks or guide sticks to make the animal come to the trap. Bait, scent, or lure can also be used as an added attraction.

Cubby Set

An old beaver hole, a large stump with the roots partially exposed, or openings between bridge timbers can be used to make a cubby or a modified cubby set for the mink. Prepare an enclosed place to fasten a bait. When the bait is solidly attached, put the trap 6 to 8 inches from the bait. Have the opening of the cubby to the water or in the direction that the mink will approach. A handful of duck or chicken feathers scattered near the front of the cubby will draw the mink's attention.

If the sets are made where there is much human activity the traps will have to be hidden deep in the brush or log jam. Water sets should all be drown sets. Otherwise traps and mink will disappear before they can be collected.

WINTER TRAPPING

Winter months in cold climates make mink trapping more difficult, but mink are also hungrier and hunt more. Ice and snow must be contended with. Make the sets at open-water riffles, under the edges of banks, by beaver dams and brush piles, and where the ice breaks near the bank. Cubby sets can also be used with good results in all of these areas.

In most areas, six to eight sets per mile will take all of the mink wanted from the area. Vary the sets as to the type of set and the bait or scent used. If the trapping is along large rivers, the number of sets may be doubled. Small meandering streams or small mountain streams should handle three or four sets a mile. Remove the traps from the area before all of the mink population are trapped. This will provide mink for next year's trapping.

KILLING AND RESETTING

To kill a mink, strike it across the head with the stick hard enough to knock it out. Use the hand or the knee to press on the heart area until it is dead. The pelt will not be damaged and it will be a quick and humane death for the animal.

If a mink is taken at a drown set, remove the mink and reset the trap. Put the set into as near natural condition as possible. Leave fresh bait if it is a bait set, fresh scent if a scent set. If it is a dry-land set and the mink was staked, there will likely be considerable set damage. Rebuild if possible, and if it is not, move the set to a new location and make a new set. The old set is best if it can be used. The caught mink will have left scent, and this will attract any new mink that comes by. Trappers who repeat in an area for succeeding years have an advantage over new trappers. They learn the set locations that are the best producers. These sets will yield mink on a continuing basis if the area is not overtrapped.

SKINNING AND FLESHING

If the trapper is running an all-day line he should skin his catches as soon as they are removed from the trap. Do not leave an unskinned mink in the sun or in a place where the pelt might get damaged. When packing the pelts, always have fur out.

Skinning a mink is a simple task. Split the inside of the rear legs from one hind foot to the other. This will put the cut forward of the anal opening and anal glands. Use care in cutting around the scent glands. Pull the hide free from the feet and hind legs. Loosen the skin from the pelvic area and down on the stomach. Loosen the hide from the base of the tail and pull the bone out. Pull the hide down to the front legs and cut free at the wrist joints. Pull on over the head and cut the ears free, skin out the eyes, and cut the lip tissue to release the hide from the carcass. Split the tail the complete length on the underside.

The fat and flesh are easiest removed if the skin is pulled onto a fleshing board. Use a small fleshing knife or an old tablespoon. Pull the front legs over the nose of the stretching board to flesh them. Wipe any free fat or grease off the pelt with a cloth or paper towel after the hide is stretched.

DRYING

The male and the female mink will vary greatly in size, so it will be best to have a separate size stretcher for each. Taper the board to fit the nose and head. Have a ¾-inch taper between the shoulders and the hips. The boards should be of ⅜-inch stock and should be 30 to 36 inches long. Shoulder width should vary from 3 to 3½ inches and hip width should be 4 to 5 inches to accept the different sizes of mink. Stretch the pelt with the fur in. Make a U-shaped area between and forward of the hind legs on the underside by pulling stomach fur forward, at the same time pulling the hip area down on the back side. This will make a window so the fur buyer can inspect the fur. Mink pelts are usually sold with the fur in and the hide out. It is not necessary to turn the fur.

If the pelts are difficult to remove from the stretching board, place a small tapered wedge between the pelt and the board when the fresh hide goes on the stretcher. All boards and wedges must have smooth edges to prevent fur damage.

Let the pelt stay on the stretcher until completely dry. Remove it from the stretcher and store it in a cool, dry, well-ventilated place until it is sold. If pelts are stacked, put a layer of paper toweling between each skin. Do not leave the hides in sunlight or in a place where they might become damp or wet. Take all carcasses back to the line the next day and dispose of them in a remote area. If the carcasses are left around the home area they will draw flies and will soon begin to stink.

17

Pine Marten

The pine marten, also sometimes called the American sable, is faster in a tree than a squirrel, as cautious as a weasel, and has the temperament of a mink. It is a graceful animal with a reddish-brown to dark-brown coat. There is a light-orange throat patch. The marten is slender and about 18 inches long. The tail is large and fluffy and may reach 10 inches. A big marten might weigh 4 pounds. Like other tree dwellers, it has sharp claws. The head is a lighter color than the rest of the body. The legs are short with large and well-furred feet. The stomach gland leaves scent on all objects touched. This marks the marten's territory.

Marten are found at high altitudes for the most part—4,000 to 10,000 feet in their southern habitats of Colorado, California, and Utah. In the northern United States and Canada they may be found at lower elevations. In parts of Canada and Alaska it is not unusual to find the pine marten near sea level.

The marten is most active at night but will at times hunt during the day if hungry or if in an area where it has not been disturbed. The hunting is done on the ground, for the most part, although it will take to the trees if the situation suggests it. In mountainous areas the marten may come to a mink set. It does not like the water as the mink does, however, and will detour around water to keep its feet dry.

The marten is most commonly found in mature stands of conifer forests. A few have adapted to cutover areas and to areas of mixed conifers and hardwoods. The home range of a marten will change from summer to winter. Food and weather conditions control these changes. The move to its summer cabin may be only a couple of miles, or it may be more than 20 miles. The marten has a two-speed transmission. It either walks or runs in a series of continuous jumps.

The main diet of the marten is the snowshoe rabbit, red-

The pine marten has well-clawed feet that make it possible for it to climb and take prey. At one time this animal was called the American sable. (*Photo: Gerry Blair*)

backed pine mouse, and little tree squirrel. Other foods sampled during the year are small reptiles, fish, birds, insects, and berries. In the winter, when food is scarce, the marten will come to any fresh meat. A dead bird or a dead rodent will attract the marten as long as the meat is not tainted.

The marten inhabits a harsh environment. To ensure survival and reproduction the marten has adapted a unique system of breeding. They mate in midsummer and the young are born the following March or April. This long gestation period results from a delayed implantation of the fertilized egg. The young are often born in a tree cavity that is many feet above the ground. The young are born blind and will open their eyes about five weeks after birth. Two weeks later they will be weaned. The young are full-grown at four months and will then strike out on their own. A two-year-old female is sexually mature and will accept a mate. Few marten will live more than about eight years.

VALUE AS A FURBEARER

Marten have been heavily trapped for many years. During the early 1900s, the fur price was high and many areas were overtrapped. Too, as virgin timber areas were logged and as land was developed, marten habitat diminished. Marten have been raised in captivity with some success. Restocking efforts have also reintroduced the marten into areas of its original range. Marten fur varies in price with size and color. At the time of this writing, prices range from $17 to $20, but in times past a good pelt might bring $50. Canada has marketed more than 60,000 marten in a single year.

TRAPS AND EQUIPMENT FOR MARTEN

The most-used trap for the marten is the No. 1 longspring. The No. 1½ longspring and the No. 1½ jump trap also work well. The smaller size of the Conibear "killer" trap is also often a good choice. The trapper will be money ahead if he uses a trap that is a little big for the marten when making sets on the ground or snow, so that other animals which are nontarget for the set but still valuable will be held when they come to the trap. Snares are also effective if the terrain lends itself to their use. An unusual marten set can be made by using horseshoe nails. A hole is drilled into the side of a tree and the sharpened nails are driven in at a 45-degree angle. When the marten pushes its head in the hole to take the bait it becomes caught on the nails and is either killed or held.

Traps for marten need no special treatment other than ensuring that they work properly. If sets are made on the side of a tree, make sure that the trap chain is well stapled, wired, or nailed to the tree. It should be easily removable, however, so that the trapper can vary the trap height as the snow level rises or lowers. Traps set at the base of a tree or at the entrance to a cubby should be staked or dragged.

Much of marten country has heavy snow during the winter months. A pair of snowshoes are almost a necessity. Extra rawhide for the lacings should be carried. A good packsack and packboard are needed. Traveling snowshoes should be narrow, long, and with a free tail part so the toe does not continually pick up snow. Bearpaw snowshoes may work well around camp but were not made as a distance shoe. Marten lines in Canada and Alaska are often run with dog teams or with snowmobiles. Before going on such a line, the marten trapper should have enough backcountry experience to stay out of trouble.

MARTEN SIGN

The main sign left by the marten is the tracks. The front and hind feet are about the same size and are slightly larger than a thumbprint. Shallow dust or soft snow will usually show footprints. In winter the bottoms of the marten's feet are heavily covered with hair. The toes and foot pad are not distinguishable in the tracks. Marten tracks are in pairs with a 1½-to-4-foot jump during normal travel. Marten droppings are about the size of mink droppings and about twice the size of weasel droppings.

The marten makes a variety of sounds. They are usually a series of low calls and are more subdued than those of other members of the weasel clan.

SETS FOR MARTEN

The marten is a curious and reckless animal. Its boldness will bring it to almost any set, even one that is poorly prepared. The tree set is the method by which most marten are caught. The cubby is also effective. Scent or lure sets are used in some areas with good results. Snares, deadfalls, and the horseshoe-nail set are seldom used.

Tree Set

The tree set is the most effective set for taking marten. Cut a tree about 4 inches in diameter and remove an 8-foot section. Lean this against a larger tree at an angle a bit more than 45 degrees. The top end should hit about 5 feet above the ground. Just above the pole contact, chop a flat surface out of the standing tree that is about a foot square. Make smooth surfaces. Staple the trap-chain ring to the north side of the tree. Leave enough loose chain so that the trap can sit an inch or two above the end of the leaning pole. With the ax make a vertical indentation where the center of the spring of the No. 1 longspring will be against the tree. Make another where the cross of the trap will be out from the tree. Make two sharp-pointed wedges about an inch square. One should be about 3 inches long and the other about 4½ inches long. Drive the shorter one into the right side; it will enter the middle of the spring opening. Drive the longer wedge in so the upper edge will be level with the bottom of the shorter wedge and centered under the bottom of the trap. The wedge through the spring should be snug, and if it isn't, readjust the size of the wedge or slide the trap to the right or left to tighten the fit. With the free jaw against the tree there is less chance of a jaw being folded over and the trap being air-snapped. If the trap is placed a foot below a large tree branch or other cover the trap will be protected from snow and ice.

Another tree set can be made by nailing a 10 x 12-inch board to the side of an open tree that does not have overhead protection. The board should be about a foot above the trap and at a slight angle. Chop a small horizontal notch where the edge of the board will fit and nail in the center edge. Nail a 1-inch branch or stick from the front outer edge of the board to the side of the tree, level or below the trap position. This will provide rain and snow protection for the set. Nail or pin the bait about 6 inches above the trap pan. If a nontarget bird or animal bothers the bait the trapper can substitute fresh fish paste. Another technique is to drill a 2 to 3-inch-diameter hole above the trap and place the bait there. A screen can be tacked over the opening to protect the bait from the nontarget animals.

The 120 or modified 220 Conibear can be used for marten. Altering the trigger wire to make it a step-on trigger below and in front of the bait makes a good set. The flattened end of the lean pole can be notched to accept the Conibear.

Above: To make a marten tree set cut a small tree and lean it at a 45-degree angle against a larger tree. The large tree should have a platter-sized piece of bark and wood removed.

Below: Nail a bait, or a pine cone with scent, about 8 inches above the angled pole.

Left: Make two vertical cuts in the large tree and drive in two wood stakes to hold the trap.
Right: Place one of the stakes through the spring of the trap and reset the trap frame on the second. Nail the trap chain to the side of the large tree. *(Photos: Gerry Blair)*

If you want the trapped animal to hang free, the trap chain can be stapled or wired a foot from the tree on the lean pole. An animal so trapped will soon die and the fur will not be damaged by small rodents.

Modified Tree Set

Cut a tree about 6 inches in diameter and about 7 feet long. Lean it against an upright tree so that about 2 feet of the leaner extends past the upright tree. Place bait or lure at the outer upper end of the leaner, nailed or wired on. Place the trap back from the bait about 6 inches and fasten the trap chain so any catch will swing free well

Above: Some trapping areas do not have trees large enough to make a tree set. To trap there, lean the pole against a standing tree so that several feet extend beyond the tree. Wire the leaner in place and wire the trap to a cut-out place. Place the bait or lure at the end of the pole.
Below: Nail the trap chain to the bottom of the leaner. The caught marten will jump for the ground and will be suspended in midair. *(Photos: Gerry Blair)*

above the ground. A Conibear can be used with this set also. It should be placed about a foot back from the bait.

This set can be used effectively in snow country. As the snow level changes, the trap is easily changed to correspond with the new ground level. The set can also be used in areas with no large trees where the standard tree set would not be possible. The set will take weasel, mink, and fisher as a bonus. Once in a while, a fox will try to steal the bait and will be caught.

Cubby Set

The cubby set varies in makeup depending on the area. The set may consist of a box built on a pole between two trees, about 4 feet off the ground, and raised as the snow level raises. The cubby may be a box shelter built to the side of a tree. If a ground cubby is used it can be placed beneath a thick evergreen and made of short sections of limbs or bark. One end of the cubby must be open to accept the trap and bait, and to allow the marten to enter. The cubby built of limbs or bark needs the support of a standing or downed tree to give it strength. Ground-level cubbies will take all furbearers. If a catch of a larger furbearer is likely, the trapper may want to go to a No. 2 longspring or a No. 2 jumper. This is a bit strong for a marten but will hold the bigger volunteers that come to the trap.

Dirt-Hole Set

Dirt-hole sets using bait or lure will take marten. The sets are made the same as the dirt-hole sets made for fox and other animals. Holes dug into the dried needle bed below the conifers are effective and are quickly made.

Auger-Hole Set

The auger-hole set was used in parts of the Northwest when traps were scarce. Use a hand auger with a 2½- or 3-inch drill to put a hole about 6 inches into the side of a tree. Put the hole about 4 feet off the ground. Make the hole on the north side of the tree. Push a chunk of fresh bait to the back of the hole. Clean the bark away from the hole lip. Sharpen until needle-sharp four horseshoe nails and drive them through the lip of the hole at an angle that lets the points rest closer than the heads. The nails should be placed so that they will catch the head of the marten when it enters the hole to take the bait. When it tries to back out the four sharp nails will pin the top and bottom of the marten's head and result in a permanent catch.

HANDLING CATCHES AND RESETTING

Few marten will remain alive in the trap until the trapper visits. They are very nervous and will fight the trap until they die of exhaustion. In very cold climates a marten will soon freeze solid if it is confined in a trap; it must keep moving to keep alive. Most marten taken here will be frozen brittle when the trapper runs the line. Their tail and legs must be warmed with the hands and then folded back against the body to prevent a break-off.

Reset the trap after the catch is removed. Check the trap chain to see that it is still well fastened. Check the bait to see that it is undisturbed, and if necessary, leave fresh bait. Use fresh lure if needed. As the snow deepens it will be necessary to raise the set to stay above the snow covering.

If a trapline is not run on a daily basis the marten fur may be cut or pulled free by small rodents for nest-building material. Many types of mice and squirrel will steal the fur. Too, if left too long, the marten may be eaten by an owl or other predator. The mice and the other fur robbers can be thwarted by making a set so that the marten hangs off the ground when it is caught. The scavengers can usually be beaten to the marten if the trapper runs his traps daily and makes his rounds as early as possible.

PELT CARE

To skin a marten, cut a slit from the inside of one hind foot to the opposite foot. Cut around the anal opening and pull the tailbone free of the tail. Slit the tail from base to tip on the underside. Remove the pelt carefully, cutting as needed. Front feet may be cut off or left on, depending on local preference. Cut the ear cartilage free from the skull, skin out the eyes, and cut the nose away from the head. Remove all excess fat and meat.

The pelt should be stretched flesh side out until it is nearly dry. Remove from the board, turn the pelt, and return it to the board. Again, if the trapper is handling a number of marten every year, it will be to his advantage to build drying boards in a size to take small, medium, and large marten. Make the boards 36 to 40 inches long. Taper the tip end to fit the marten's head. A medium skin would need a board that measured 3 inches across at a point 8 inches below the tip; 30 inches below the tip the board should measure 4 inches. Make the board slightly larger for the big marten and slightly smaller for the peewee.

18
Raccoon

The raccoon is a heavy-bodied animal with short legs. Adults will reach a body length of 18 to 28 inches with another 10 inches of tail. A young adult will weigh about 12 pounds and an old boar may get up to 35 pounds. The body fur will be mostly dark in the Pacific states and light in the more desert areas. Throughout the remainder of the range, the raccoon will show a grizzled gray with the familiar black face mask. The tail is ringed with alternating bands of yellowish white and black.

The raccoon has increased its range as a result of land development in the western United States and Canada. The predator-control projects in Montana, Wyoming, Utah, and Idaho have encouraged raccoon expansion. As the larger predators such as the coyote and the wolf were thinned, the territory opened up for the smaller raccoon. The coon is an adaptable animal; it can exist very near and at times within large cities and do very well.

The raccoon prefers range that has a good supply of water. Marshes, riverbanks, and lake borders are all potential raccoon hotspots. Heavy timber, brushy canyons, slide rock areas, old farm buildings, and deserted beaver lodges will also hold good raccoon numbers. They range from sea level to more than 8,000 feet. They are sometimes caught in a trap set miles from water intended to catch bobcat or coyote.

The raccoon prefers a large hole or a hollow tree for the main winter den. The young are also born and raised here. The breeding activity takes place in late winter. About two months later the young are born, usually in early spring. The average litter is four. The females sometimes accept the male at one year of age but will more commonly wait until their second year when they are mature. The young will stay with the mother until late summer or early fall.

In early fall, when the nights begin to show a promise of

Although he is primarily known as a water animal the raccoon is often found many miles from the nearest water. (Photo: Gerry Blair)

winter, the coon will begin a frantic eating spree to put on fat for winter. The raccoon is omnivorous, eating both plants and animals, and will gorge on berries, fruits, corn, nuts, insects, amphibians, fish, birds, small mammals, the meat of large mammals, and garbage.

In cold climates, the raccoon may crawl into a hole or a hollow tree and sleep part of the winter. Any warm spell will bring it out of this hibernation, however, and it will leave the den to seek out food to replace its depleted layer of fat. In lower altitudes or warmer climate, the raccoon will not hibernate but will feed nightly year-round.

The raccoon is a good swimmer and climbs trees about as well as any animal around. When full-grown it is a good fighter, and if it cannot run, swim, or climb from danger will stand and fight. These abilities allow the raccoon to escape from about everything that might threaten it.

HARMFUL EFFECTS

The raccoon will not do great damage around the farm or ranch unless their numbers get out of hand. In areas of raccoon over-population, however, great damage occurs. If there is a lack of natural food, the raccoon will turn to domestic crops with gusto. A few coon will wipe out a cornfield, a garden, or an orchard in short order. They will also take domestic fowl.

VALUE AS A FURBEARER

The raccoon pelt is a staple of the fur industry. There will be years of high demand, and when this happens, the value of the pelts will increase. The pelt is almost always worth skinning and handling. If the trapper catches the raccoon, either as a target or nontarget animal, he should keep and handle the fur. The fur is prime from November until the last of February through most of the range. Many trappers retain the carcass of the raccoon for table fare. Cleaned and roasted, it will make an excellent meal.

TRAPS AND EQUIPMENT FOR RACCOON

The No. 1½ longspring, the No. 1½ coilspring, and the No. 1½ underspring are all good raccoon traps. The No. 11 is also good. It is stronger for its size but has a smaller jaw spread. Some trappers will use a strong No. 1 when they are short on the No. 1½. A large coon, however, will often pull out of the No. 1 and a fur will be lost. No. 2 traps can be used for raccoon but the trapper will lose some animals from twist-off. The trap is a bit strong for the raccoon and often breaks the leg. The coon will then twist on out of the trap. Either a No. 2 or a No. 3 will work fine in drown sets.

The 220 Conibear is also a good raccoon trap. It is a kill set and any coon taken will stay in the trap. Do not use the Conibear, however, in areas where nontarget animals are likely to come to the set. In many areas, hunters use dogs to run raccoons at night. Keep the Conibear away from these areas as it will kill a coonhound as readily as a coon.

If you are working in shallow water a good pair of rubber boots will be needed to trap the raccoon. Use knee boots or hip boots depending on the water depth. You also need sidecutters, either 8- or 10-inch, a hatchet, trowel, trapping wire, extra gloves, a light canvas, and a gunny sack or two to carry the catch in. Bait and scent are also needed but should not come in contact with the traps. If stakes are used, prepare them from a hardwood such as oak and drive them in with a hatchet. The chain should be short when the trap is staked.

Drags of any type can be used for coon. They must be heavy enough, however, to keep the raccoon near the set. The coon is a powerful animal for its size and can pull a light drag a long way. Whenever possible use a drown set for the raccoon. Make the set with weights and a drowning wire just as you would in beaver trapping.

If the raccoon set is made on dry land, and in country where it is likely to take a fox, make the set as you would for the fox. Use a wax-paper pan cover and conceal the trap. If the trap is strictly for raccoon the wax paper is not needed. Many trappers place the bare trap in shallow water and wrap the pan with aluminum foil as an attractor.

RACCOON SIGN

Raccoon tracks are often seen in the mud of stream banks or lake edges. In dry country, the tracks are sometimes found in the dust of the trail. Snow-country tracks are easy to see. The front foot of the coon is much smaller than the rear foot. The rear footprint will somewhat resemble the track of a small child. Claw marks are usually visible.

If there are large trees in the area, check all hollow trees for denning activity. There will be coon hair caught on the bark. There will also be a lot of droppings near the base of the tree. Do not cut or damage den trees. If left unmolested the den trees will provide a good supply of raccoon in the area for many seasons. Look for parts of crayfish, fish, frogs, or corn ears that have been partially eaten. Near the den the raccoon will often leave visible trails leading to the feeding area.

If the trapper is not familiar with the trapping area, he should look for sign near marshes, large brush piles, old beaver-dam areas, abandoned buildings, areas with large broken rock, badger holes, hawk nests, and bridges or culverts. The trapper may save scouting time by becoming friendly with the local landowners. Often they will be able to report areas of raccoon concentration.

SETS FOR RACCOON

The dirt-hole set will take raccoon. Like most other predators, the raccoon is an opportunist. If it believes that another animal has hidden away a part of its lunch, the raccoon will do its best to take it. The dirt-hole set for raccoon can be made in any one of a number of ways including in open areas, ground-den holes, water pockets, and stump holes.

Stump-Hole Set

The stump-hole set can be made in a rotten stump with a 6-to-10-inch-diameter hole dug at the base. A hand auger can also be used to drill a hole 6 to 8 inches into the stump. Incline the hole slightly upward to keep water out of it.

The raccoon likes to check the face of dead stumps and dead trees. A rotten stump can be used as a set site by making a hole in the dead wood at ground level. Make the hole 4 inches in diameter and about 8 inches into the stump. Tear up the ground a foot or two at the base of the stump so the raccoon will be attracted to the set. Put the bait at the rear of the hole. Dig out a cavity for the trap in front of the bait hole. Tie down with a stake or a drag. If a stake is used the coon will do a lot of digging at the site and the trap will have to be moved to a new set. Cover the trap and chain with rotten leaves or wood and the set is finished. Use fresh meat, canned sardines, burnt honey with apples, fish heads, or parts of a chicken for bait.

Another variation of the stump set is the hole drilled into the side of the stump. The hole should be at least an inch in diameter. Slant the hole slightly upward to prevent water accumulation. Start the hole about 6 inches above ground level. Push the bait to the rear of the hole. The trap can be stapled to the tree, staked, or fastened to a drag. If a handful of feathers are scattered at the stump base or a small amount of lure placed a few inches above the bait hole, every raccoon that passes will come to investigate. Set the trap about 4 inches back from the stump in line with the bait hole. Dig the set in, and if fox, coyote, or bobcat run in the area, use a wax-paper pan cover and conceal the trap with a thin layer of soil.

Quick Dirt-Hole Set

A dirt-hole set that is fast to make can be a real coon taker. Dig a 4-inch-diameter hole about a foot into the ground. Do not .dig straight down; angle the hole slightly. The hole should be near a trail, a fence row, or a ditch that shows raccoon travel. Place the bait at the back of the hole. Tie a drag made from a branch several inches thick and 5 or 6 feet long to the trap chain. An 8- to 10-pound rock or piece of metal also makes a good drag. To make sets fast the trapper should carry a half-dozen wooden stakes about 2 feet long in the trap pack. In areas where no natural drags are obvious the trapper will not waste time in hunting a suitable drag. He can stake instead.

Place the trap by digging a suitable hole. Put the trap about 4 inches in front of the bait hole and about 2 inches off center. Cover the trap with leaves or dead grass. If other animals are in the area, use a wax-paper pan cover and conceal the trap with dirt. Tie down to a stake or a drag. About every third set use a few drops of commercial lure. Vary the bait used from trap to trap. Some old coons develop a preference for a particular bait.

Den Set

If a hole is being used by a raccoon as a den, tie the trap chain to a drag that cannot be pulled into the hole. This is a good place to use fish oil or lure. Dig the trap in and cover it lightly with dead grass or leaves. If the den will be damaged to any extent, make the set back a short distance from the den opening. If a trail can be identified leading away from the den, make the set there. Put the set just off the trail and on the side where the prevailing wind will carry the odor of the bait or lure to the trail.

Water-Pocket Dirt-Hole Set

Use a trowel or a small shovel to dig a hole in a steep bank about 12 inches in diameter. The hole should be about 6 inches above the water level and extend into the bank 14 or so inches. Pile the loose dirt from the hole in front of the bait hole and let some of the dirt fall down into the water. Use a No. 1½ trap rigged with a drowning wire and slide lock. A drag can also be used. Tie a 12-pound weight to the trap chain. A 220 Conibear can also work here. Set the trap at the water's edge and stake in position.

Fish, fish oil, or a muskrat carcass is good bait. Place it at the rear of the hole. A few drops of raccoon lure placed at the lip of the hole will add to the set.

Sets of this type are often taken by trap thieves. If using a steel trap, dig in and cover with moss or leaves. Cover any visible chain or wire. Put grass or dry leaves loosely over the bait, also to hide it from sight. This set will also take mink.

Blind Set

The blind set is made with no attractor. To be effective, it must be placed on a trail that is regularly used by raccoons. A trail that leads from the den to a feeding area is the best bet. Seasonal travel on trails leading to a cornfield, an orchard, a berry patch, or a marshy area are all good possibilities. Look for tracks or for weed trails. Lay a drag stick across the trail. It will serve as a drag for the trap and as a natural stepping stick. Dig the trap in and place it with the jaws parallel with the trail. The trap pan should be 3 or 4 inches back of the step stick. Cover the trap and the chain with loose leaves or grass. Put a few drops of fish oil on a tuft of grass beside the trail. A drop or two of raccoon lure will also work. It is not now strictly a blind set, but the few drops of lure might bring in the big boar of the territory.

Shiny-Pan Set

The raccoon is a curious animal and is constantly looking for something to eat. It will pick up and handle any shiny object. Many coons have been taken using nothing but a can lid or a piece of aluminum foil over the trap pan as an attractor.

This set is best used when it is made in the water. Put the trap or traps in water 2 to 6 inches deep and near the bank. Wrap aluminum foil around the pan. Lure can be placed on the bank if desired to act as a call for passing coon. The set works best if it is placed in the shallow water below a vertical bank. Rig the trap as a drowner if the water depth permits. If this is not possible, use a drag to allow the coon to pull away from the water and hide in the nearby cover.

Cubby Set

There are many types of cubby sets. It may be a box type that is open at one end. Some cubbies have a leaning pole to form the overhang. Others utilize the V formed from two windfalls. The natural cubby is the fastest to set up. Find a log jam or brush pile or form branches into a V. With a little adjustment, the trapper can force the coon to pass the trap on its way to the bait. Nail the bait or wire it so that it cannot be picked up and carried away. Cover the trap with leaves. The trap should be about 6 inches back from the bait. Fasten the trap to a drag so that the caught coon will not destroy the set. All of the cubby sets are essentially the same. A natural or constructed "cubby hole" has bait at the back and a trap at the front. The sets can be simple or complex. Some trappers make a box open at one end, and make the sets well before trapping season begins. When the season opens they come to the sets and place the traps. They save time this way and will end up with more fur at season's end.

Culvert Set

The culvert with or without water is a natural travelway for the raccoon. Some culvert sets are not legal as they are too close to a road. Check the local trapping laws before making the set. If the set is legal, put the trap at the lowest end of the culvert and use coon lure or fish oil as an attractor. It is generally best to use a drag unless a drowning set is possible. The culvert set should be checked daily and as soon after dawn as possible. It is a strong temptation for any trap thief that may come by.

Bridge Set

Bridges crossing large or small streams are also natural travelways for raccoons. There will be natural crossings here, and often a den, log jams, holes between bridge timbers, and natural shelter. Here again, check the local trapping regulations to make sure that the law allows such a set. Hide the set as well as possible to stymie the trap thief. Check the set early in the day, every day. Make the set as a dirt-hole set, a trail set, or a cubby. The shiny-pan set will work well here too, but make the set at the edge of the bridge so that the moonlight will have a chance to light up the attractor. Use a drowner if possible. A killer trap works well here too, but the trapper takes a chance of losing a valuable trap to thieves, as the Conibear is more easily seen than the steel trap. The trapper will collect a bonus if the trap is made on back-country roads. Mink, weasel, and skunk will come to the trap as well as raccoon. Occasionally a bobcat or fox will be caught.

KILLING AND RESETTING

If the set is a drowner, the raccoon will be dead when the trapper arrives. Otherwise the trapper should use care in handling the coon. They are strong and they are fighters. Hit the coon across the forehead with the kill stick and use your knee or foot to give a hard blow just back of the front leg. Repeat several times. This kills quickly with no suffering. A coon can be killed with a severe blow to the head but there is a likelihood that the nose will bleed and make it necessary to wash the fur. The raccoon can also be shot with a .22 using a CB cartridge. Put the shot just above and between the eyes.

Reset the trap. If blood from the raccoon is on the ground or snow, remove it. The odor left by a trapped animal will often bring another in more readily. The blood, however, is a warning that danger exists there. Do not waste time at the set. If a long line is being tended you must kill the animal quickly, reset without being messy, and go on to the next trap. If the line is being tended by vehicle, you should not skin the animals on the line. Take them home and do the job there. If the line is a foot line, you will not want to carry a heavy coon too far. Skin it out as quickly as possible and go to the next trap.

When the coon has been killed and removed from the trap the skin must be protected from damage. Carry a gunny sack or two to carry the pelt or unskinned coon. If the weather is warm, do not delay the skinning too long. In a matter of hours the carcass will taint. Keep the raccoon away from the direct sun as this speeds up the process of tissue breakdown.

SKINNING
Raccoon are fat and greasy. Skin the animals out of doors, and if that is not possible, pick an indoor locality that will be easy to clean. Slit the inside of the rear legs from foot to foot. Cut around the anal opening. Split open the tail on the underside and remove the bone. Cut the skin loose at the heel of each hind foot. Use a tie rope or a metal hook to suspend the coon at a comfortable working height. Free the skin from the hips and continue skinning down to the front legs. Cut the skin loose at each wrist and remove the front legs. Work on down to the ears and cut the ear cartilage loose from the skull. Skin out the eyes. Work the skin down over the snout and cut loose at the nose.

FLESHING, DRYING, AND STRETCHING
Pull the pelt onto a fleshing board or a beam with the flesh side out. Use a fleshing knife and a scraper to remove all flesh and fat.

Wipe the hide free of any oily fat left. The hide can be washed with warm water and soap if desired. Wipe the hide with a cotton cloth or paper towels to remove the last of the grease.

Pull the hide onto the stretcher with the fur side in and nail the rear of the hide to the board. Nail the spread tail from top to bottom to get a tight stretch. Put the nails about an inch apart, so that the tail is held open to dry properly. Pull the hind legs down on the stomach side and nail in place. Use a tapered stick between the hide and the board to make it possible to remove the hide when it comes time to take it from the stretcher. Push up the center of the stomach skin to make a U-shaped inspection window. This will cause a thickening of the stomach fur and will make it easier for the fur grader to work the pelt. Raccoon skins are sold fur side in and the inspection window allows the grader a look at the fur of the hips. The lower lip should be tacked to the board. The front leg skins hang, but should not touch the skin of the chest; stand the stretcher at an angle so the skin of the legs hangs free. When the pelt has dried, remove it from the board and hang it from a nail or a hook in a well-ventilated and cool area.

If any number of raccoon are caught yearly, the trapper should have at least three sizes of stretchers—one for the large coon, one for medium, and one for small. A suggested length would be 40 inches. The board width should be 8 inches at the base and 5½ inches at the shoulders for a small coon, 6½ and 9 inches for a medium, and 7½ and 10 inches for a large. To get the shoulder measurement, go down about 12 inches from the point of the board.

CONSERVATION
Do not trap all of the raccoon from an area. Leave some to serve as breeders for the coming season. If small young coon are caught and are not injured, the trapper might want to release them and let them grow for next year's trapping. Do not molest or destroy den trees. If a specific raccoon is doing damage in a particular area, and it is during the summer, live-trap the animal and release it at a distant part of the trapping area. Inform all landowners of your trapping and the locations of sets, and assist them with any problems they may have with predation. The trapper must have the support of the landowner if he is to enjoy trapping on a continuing basis.

19
Weasel

The weasel is a very efficient predator. In spite of its small size it is able to take and eat much larger animals with monotonous regularity. This small killer is known in North America by its three subspecies: the long-tailed, the short-tailed (ermine), and the least weasel. The long-tailed weasel is the biggest of the bunch and will tip the scales at a whopping 8 ounces. A big one will measure about 2 feet in length. The short-tailed weasel grows over 13 inches long and weighs about 4 ounces. The least weasel is usually under 8 inches and will weigh 2 ounces.

The weasel is one of the few furbearers that has a coat for each season, brown in summer and white in winter. This practical adaptation is triggered by the lengthening or shortening of the day or night. The trapping laws in most states restrict trapping except when the white coat is present. In some parts of its southern range, probably due to survival selectivity, the weasel remains a shade of brown the year around.

The weasel is found in one or another of its subspecies in most of the North American states and in Canada, and in a closely related subspecies through most of Europe. It is also found in Northern and Central Asia.

The weasel breeds in midsummer. Through delayed implantation, the young begin development the following spring and are born in early summer. Four to ten young are the average litter. The young develop rapidly and are eating solid food within three weeks. At two months of age the kits hunt with the parent. The young continue this rapid development and reach mature size by the fall.

The weasel is a territorial animal. It uses a ground squirrel hole, a rotten log, or a crevice in a rock pile as a main den. It will return to the same den after a night's hunting, or if the hunt takes it too far afield, in a matter of a few days. The big weasels may have a

A hollow log makes an excellent site for trapping the long-tailed weasel. *(Photo: Leonard Lee Rue III)*

hunting territory of a square mile. The smaller members of the clan may limit their hunting to a couple of acres.

In winter the weasel travels extensively through the snow and may extend its range due to a shortage of food. Usually weasel tracks are plentiful in these restricted hunting forays along all stream banks and from brush patch to brush patch.

Mice, rats, and ground squirrels are the main diet of the weasel. Its appetite is insatiable. If its stomach is so full that it can't eat another bite it will find a hole to sleep a short time. Its high metabolism, however, soon consumes the food and it is forced to hunt again. To stay alive, the weasel must hunt, kill, and eat almost continuously. The long-tailed weasel kills rabbits, chickens, and ducks. The kill may be so large that the weasel is unable to drag it. It must make its meal at the kill site, and most of the time leave the bulk of the kill to some other predator. If there is snow on the ground and the kill is easier to drag, long furrows may appear in the snow indicating that the weasel has taken its lunch to a less public place.

HARMFUL EFFECTS
The long-tailed weasel is well known to many who raise poultry. It has an uncanny ability to squeeze through small openings and gain access to the chicken coop. Once entry is gained, the weasel might kill a dozen or more chickens in one short killing orgy. It will continue to return to the coop night after night until it is caught and killed. Young domestic rabbits are also a tasty dish for the weasel, and it has a taste for the young of all game birds and the smaller game animals. To balance the ledger somewhat, the weasel is an efficient predator of the small rodents that often plague the farmer.

TRAPS FOR WEASEL
The No. 0 longspring is the trap best suited for weasel. In areas where other slightly larger furbearers are apt to be caught the No. 1 longspring or No. 1 jumper might be a better choice. It is a bit large for the weasel but will take and hold the occasional mink, marten, or skunk that volunteers to the trap. The No. 1½ can be used for weasel if it is set as a killer trap. Raise the free jaw and set the pan for hair-trigger release. The weasel will be forced over the trigger jaw and under the free jaw and will be instantly killed. Box traps will also work well on weasel. The drawbacks of size, cost, and possible theft limit their use.

WEASEL SIGN
The weasel leaves a great number of tracks when snow is on the ground. The least weasel has a foot that is about ¼ inch across. Its jumps will cover 4 to 8 inches. The tracks will be side by side. The short-tailed weasel normally jumps 6 to 12 inches, and the long-tailed weasel may take jumps of 12 to 24 inches. Weasel travel is usually by jumping. The walking tracks will be seen mostly around a denning area. Weasel tracks are quite similar to mink tracks. They are much smaller, however, and will not ordinarily be found around the water as much as is true of mink. Weasel droppings are about 1½ inches long, slender, and dark colored.

Look for the droppings around ground-squirrel holes, by brush piles, and on the edges of rock piles.

WEASEL SETS

The cubby, the tree set, and the dirt-hole set will all take weasel. Their continual hunger, and their curiosity, make them easy to trap. They will come readily to any fresh meat bait. Rabbit is a good bait; so are parts of a chicken, duck, or rodent.

Cubby Set

If a cubby is made to take the weasel selectively, make the cubby no larger than a quart-sized container. An effective cubby can be made using an empty 2-quart milk carton, an empty juice can, or any empty container of similar size. Put the bait in the back of the can. Set a No. 0 or No. 1 trap near the entrance. The bait is protected from the weather and from the sight of possible bait robbers. The weasel is led over the trap on its way to the bait. The entire unit can be easily hidden below a log or in a brush pile. The trap can be staked or fastened too. Use about a 6-pound weight if a drag is used. The set may take a fox or a bobcat occasionally. With the small traps, the volunteer is not likely to stay held. The use of a drag increases the trapper's chance of holding this unexpected bonus.

The cubby can also be made from wood or bark. Make it beside a windfall, in front of a stump, or below a bank. All of these areas are natural hunting areas for the weasel. A meat bait or fish oil will bring the weasel to the trap.

Dirt-Hole Set

Dig a hole into the edge of a dirt bank, beneath a log, or at the base of a stump. Make the hole about 4 inches in diameter and a foot deep. Push a piece of bait to the back of the hole and set the trap at the opening. If fox or other predators are likely to come to the set, take extra care in finishing the set. Dig the trap in, cover with a pan cover or leaves, and use rubber gloves and a kneeling tarp when making the set. Adjust the pan tension so that the trap will spring with very light pressure. A weasel is light-footed and may weigh only a few ounces. If the pan is set too hard the weasel will pass through without springing the trap and will have a free lunch at the trapper's expense.

Ground-squirrel holes that have been abandoned, old badger

A milk-carton set for weasel. The small predators often prowl these log piles.
(Photo: Gerry Blair)

holes, and old woodchuck holes are easily converted to a natural-appearing dirt-hole set.

HANDLING TRAPPED WEASEL

The weasel is generally dead by the time the trapper arrives the next day. It is a hyperactive animal and will fight the trap until it dies of nervous exhaustion. If one is found alive it can be quickly killed by tapping it lightly on the head with the kill stick and pressing with the hand against the side of the chest. A weasel is small, but it is lightning-fast and has sharp teeth. As with all trapped animals, be very careful. Do not allow any of the oil-like scent of the weasel to touch the hands or clothing. The smell is

repulsive and lasts a long time. Reset the trap and return the set to
its original appearance.

In the colder areas the trapped weasel may be frozen solid and
the feet may be curved around the trap. Do not force the weasel out
of the trap. The limbs are brittle when they are frozen and will
likely break, causing fur damage. Warm the limbs slightly with
your hands until they are pliable. Use care when removing the
frozen animal from the trap and in transporting it. Thaw the tail
slightly by hand warming and bend it up against the belly.

PELT CARE

Most of the time the weasel is white when trapped. Put the animal
in a place where the fur will not be soiled. Before skinning, thaw
any frozen weasel. Split the inside of the rear legs from pad to pad.
Trim around the scent glands located near the anal opening. Free
the skin from the legs by cutting at the ankles, or if preferred, cut
off the rear feet. Pull the tailbone free and peel the hide down over
the body. Cut free from the front feet. Cut the ear cartilage from the
skull. Skin out the eyes and the snout and cut the nose to free the
pelt. Split the tail on the underside to ensure drying.

Weasels are not normally fat and do not usually require fleshing. Put the pelt directly on the drying board. Make the board a
foot long for the ermine weasel. It should be 2 inches wide at the
base and about 1¼ inches wide at the shoulders. The front of the
board should be tapered to fit the head. For the long-tailed weasel
the board should measure 2 inches at the shoulders and 3 inches at
the hips. Increase the board length to 2 feet. The boards should be
³/₁₆-inch stock with the edges rounded and smooth. A thin
stomach wedge may be used to make it easier to remove the skin
when dry. Use two small nails in each hind foot and one at the base
of the tail to hold the pelt in place. All weasel should be dried with
the fur in. Keep the pelt away from sun or any warm area. When
the pelt is dry, remove it from the board and store it by laying flat
or by hanging it from a string run through the eyes.

20
Wolverine

The wolverine is the largest member of the weasel family in North America. It has a bad temper, and along with it an ability to discharge a foul-smelling musk that makes everyone around leave the area. The wolverine is a chunky, short-set animal. Body length is about 3 feet, and weight, on the average, about 30 pounds. The fur is dark brown with a lighter-brown strip along the sides. The wolverine is inordinately strong when one considers the size of the animal.

The wolverine mates during early summer, but through delayed implantation the female egg does not start developing until fall or winter, and the two or three young are born the following spring. The young are lighter than the adult, with fur shading more to a cream than a brown. The den may be a hollow log, a cave, a log pile, or any available shelter.

The young stay at the den with the mother for eight weeks. They are then introduced to solid food, and will start traveling with the mother in quest of food. They are about two-thirds grown by fall and are ready to strike out on their own.

The wolverine is always hungry. It will eat anything from a mouse to a moose. The mouse is easier to catch and kill, so it makes up the main part of the diet. Other rodents, such as chipmunk, rabbit, and ground squirrel, are also taken. So are ptarmigan. The wolverine will even eat insects and berries, and will gorge itself on a carcass with considerable gusto. When a dead or dying moose, caribou, elk, or deer is found the wolverine will usually set up camp on the spot and will not resume its travels until the bones are picked clean. A larger predator, such as a bear or wolf, that makes a kill is likely to be run off by the wolverine. The carcass is then claimed and bones cleaned by the new owner. The wolverine has more fight than sense, and most of the predators, unless they happen to be near starvation, will not tangle with it over a piece of meat.

The wolverine has a temper that would make a junkyard dog envious. Most of the tales about it, though, are pure fiction. It is not hard to trap.

The wolverine is found over most of Canada, in Alaska, and in many parts of the Rocky Mountain states. A few may have returned to Minnesota and Pennsylvania. During the last twenty years the wolverine has increased in numbers and has repopulated much of its original habitat. In Montana, for example, to catch or see sign of a wolverine was unusual between 1900 and 1960, but in the ten years between 1967 and 1977, more than 200 wolverine were sold in the state.

The wolverine is surrounded by more myths and old wives' tales than any other furbearer. The stories get taller as the barroom trapper downs more liquor. Experienced trappers, however, in their sober moments know that the wolverine is a dumb furbearer. It is certainly easier to trap than smart animals like the wolf, coyote, or red fox. The bear is the worst offender in cabin damage and not the wolverine. Most cabin damage, in old as well as modern times, is caused by tree squirrels, mice, and rats. The wolverine is often accused of following the trapper's line to eat and destroy his entire catch and traps. Actually, the otter is a much worse thief on the mink and muskrat trapline than the wolverine. The coyote and mountain lion account for more damaged fur than the wolverine. As for brains, many wolverine have been caught in sets where the traps were not even covered. Often, if a wolverine is feeding in an area, it will be caught the first or second night the traps are out.

Most states, it should be noted, now protect the wolverine or have a controlled season. The animal deserves total protection in most of its range. With protection, it should soon come back to its former numbers and will again be an important North American furbearer.

WOLVERINE SIGN

The wolverine does not hibernate and must forage throughout the winter to stay alive. It is a continual traveler during the winter months as it searches out a daily living. The carcasses of big-game animals that have been winter-killed make up much of its diet. The track of the wolverine is somewhat bearlike but is much smaller. The track has five toes and a pad that does not usually leave a total imprint. The front foot is a bit larger than the rear. Claw imprints are usually visible from all feet. A big track might be 4 inches across. The sign most often seen is the deep trough made as the short-legged wolverine wallows in deep snow.

TRAPS AND SETS FOR WOLVERINE

There are recorded instances where a wolverine has come to a marten set and become hung in a No. 1 longspring. Holding this strong animal in so light a trap is uncommon. A No. 2 trap is the absolute minimum a trapper should use for the wolverine. He will have better luck holding the catch if the No. 3 longspring or No. 3 underspring jump trap is used. Many experienced trappers, when they set a trap that is specifically aimed at the wolverine, will use nothing lighter than a No. 4.

Cubby Set

The baited cubby is the most effective set to take the wolverine. Back the set by putting it against a good-sized tree. Use limbs or small poles to make the sides and the top. The entrance should be about a foot square. Fasten the bait at the back end of the cubby.

Dig the traps in and lightly cover them with rotting pine needles or snow. The wolverine will readily come to bait when it is hungry, and it is always hungry. Tie the trap to a drag that weighs at least 20 pounds. Use the drag, because the wolverine is strong and will tear up the set badly if it is staked or tied down.

The same set can be made by using a Conibear 330. Put the trap about a foot in front of the bait. Bend two-thirds of the trigger wires straight forward so that they will be stepped on by the wolverine on its way to the bait. Fasten the trap with a stick through both spring rings. Have a stick with several short branch stubs at the big end. Poke the small end through the spring rings with the spring ends pointing down. Have the bait wired about a foot above the ground. Fix the cubby poles so that the wolverine cannot detour around the trap. If the stakes are driven through each spring ring separately and into the ground, deep snow, or loose pine needles, there will be less chance of the wolverine twisting out of the trap.

Snowshoe-Trail Set

The wolverine soon learns that the trapper's snowshoe trail is the easiest place to walk. Trails left by snowmobiles or dog sleds are also natural walkways for the wolverine. Other animals such as the coyote, the fox, the mountain lion, and the wolf also use these wilderness walkways. The trapper will do well to inspect these trails at regular intervals to learn what type of critters are following the trapline trail. If a few extra traps are carried in the pack, the trapper can pick up a bonus animal now and then by making a bait or scent set along the trail.

KILLING A CATCH

When a wolverine is caught the trapper should note carefully how well the animal is secured in the trap. If it is well caught, use the kill stick to deliver a solid blow just above the eyes. If you carry a .22 pistol or rifle on the line you might be better off to shoot the wolverine between and just above the eyes with a .22 Short. Do not take chances with the wolverine. It is strong and it is cranky. The bite can be just as severe as that of a timber wolf. When the catch is removed, reset the trap, for the odor left in the area will attract any other wolverine that comes within smelling distance.

PELT CARE

Skin the wolverine the same as you would a raccoon. Skin out the front and hind feet and leave the claws on the hide, as many pelts are sold for wall mounts. When the fur has been skinned down to the claws they can be snipped from the toebones of the foot by using a pair of diagonal cutters or cutting at the last toe joint.

Split the hide from one hind foot to the front edge of the anal opening. Continue cutting to the opposite hind foot. Do not puncture the scent gland that is located near the anal opening. Split the tail on the underside and remove the tailbone. Leave all of the hide and toes of the hind feet on the skin. Tie the carcass by the hind legs and suspend it at a comfortable working height. Skin on down to the front legs and totally skin them out. Again, leave the pad and the claws on the skin. Continue skinning to the ears and cut the ear cartilage loose from the skull. Skin around the eyes, lips, and nose and cut the hide loose from the skull.

Most wolverines are fat. Remove all excess fat and any meat by using a fleshing beam and a scraper.

Pull the pelt, hair side in, over a stretcher that is about the size used for bobcat or coyote. Put a small board crossways on the two-piece stretcher about the tail area. Nail the hind legs down and spread the stretcher to the desired width. Secure the stretcher in this position by using a crosspiece. Tack on the tail board and nail the back of the hide and the tail in place. Use hand soap and lukewarm water to wash the leather side of the hide. This will remove loose fat and oil.

Hang the hide in a cool, dry place until it is nearly dry, remove it from the stretcher, and turn it so that the fur side is out. Put back on the stretcher and nail in position. Leave the hide on the stretcher until it is totally dry. Remove, comb the fur, and hang the pelt by the nose in a cool, dry place.

21
Otter

The river otter is one of the larger members of the weasel family. It is well adapted to a life in water and on land. The otter is a long slender animal with a body 26 to 36 inches long and a heavy tail 12 to 17 inches long. Weight varies from 10 to 35 pounds. The female is slightly smaller than the male. The upper parts are dark brown in color; underparts are paler and often have a silvery sheen. The lower jaw and throat are a whitish color. The otter has small ears and a broad snout. The feet are webbed, and the tail is thick at the base, tapering to the tip. The river otter is found in Alaska, through most of Canada, throughout the U.S., and from Mexico to Panama.

Otter remain near water most of the time. They are great travelers, covering a stream course for 50 to 60 miles in making the rounds of their territory. Otter are excellent swimmers. They live principally on fish and crayfish, but frogs, turtles, birds, and small mammals make up a small part of their diet.

Otter will move from area to area—they are where you find them and not necessarily where their old droppings are. Otter droppings contain a great amount of fish scales. A common toilet location may be used, causing an accumulation of fish scales.

In many areas where there are steep banks the otter will form slideways for playing. In snow and icy habitat they are continually sliding down banks, racing, and sliding under the snow. During the summer in the Northern habitat and year round in the Central and Southern states otter will form trails where they leave and enter the water. Beaver and otter are compatible. The dams and holes make a natural habitat for the otter. Otter follow set patterns and travel routes. Other otter often follow the same routes and trails when new to the place.

Otter are strong animals, pulling out of small traps with little trouble. Larger predators look them over but let them alone.

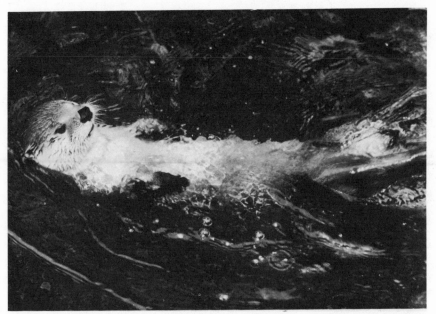

The otter will often swim belly up and will feed in this position. *(Photo: Gerry Blair)*

In breeding season a male may travel overland for many miles. The last of February 1938, a large otter crossed from the West Fork of the Bitterroot River, over a divide, and down Cooper Creek to the Selway River. This was a distance of over 30 miles of frozen small streams and a divide about 8,000 feet in elevation covered with 16 feet of snow.

The breeding cycle is usually during the summer, fall, and early winter. Gestation varies from nine to over twelve months after breeding. Delayed implantation undoubtedly takes place, for after egg development starts it is about sixty-three days before the young are born during March or April. One to four young is the average. The otter does not dig its own den; it may use an old beaver hole, a cavity under a tree stump, or a space under a log jam. The young are taught to swim, and remain with the parent until fall. They hunt, play, and travel as a group, with the adult always in charge. At about eight months the young will disband. The young often leave in pairs looking for a new place to live.

If an otter becomes angered it releases musk. When alarmed it makes a coughing noise. When angered or hurt it makes a scream-

Most of the otter's diet comes from the water. It eats fish, crayfish, frogs, salamanders, muskrat, ducks, and rabbit. *(Photo: Gerry Blair)*

ing noise as the mink or weasel does. An otter when contented and happy will emit a chirp or low chuckle.

Many otter are kept as pets, but even though they are bright and generally friendly they are a one-owner animal. They are short-tempered, can bite severely, and are very strong.

Otter have been reintroduced into areas where they were exterminated due to pollution, disease, and trapping.

The otter may kill an occasional muskrat or duck but they are not known to be destructive. Along the Pacific Coast, some salmon are caught and eaten. Because the otter is limited in number the few game fish they eat is no great problem.

VALUE AS A FURBEARER
Otter fur is at its peak from the last of November till the last of February. Many are caught in beaver sets through March. The average price for otter the winter of 1977-78 was $45. In a single trapping season, Canada has harvested 18,000, Washington 800, and Oregon 300; Alaska varied from year to year with lows of 1,000 and highs of 4,000. This seems to be a stable harvest. With any extensive drop in the yearly catch, there would be controls set by the different states or provinces.

OTTER SIGN

Otter are unpredictable as to how long they stay in an area, when they will come back, and what direction they take when leaving. You might have the good luck of finding some otter that are satisfied to remain in a small territory. Otter when traveling have a set pattern. Even other otter coming into the area seem to pick up the same travel pattern. Watch for their tracks in mud along lakes, open-water marshes, rivers, and streams. When the area is frozen and snowed in, the otter will come out at riffles, beaver dams, and any open water. They will travel in the snow. When walking, their tracks are in a slight zigzag pattern. When they jump, their hind feet and then their front feet are side by side and the paired tracks 20 to 40 inches apart.

In the snow they will run and slide. They may do this for miles when crossing between rivers and lakes in the wintertime. Near open water if banks are covered with snow they are continually playing. Watch for areas along a bank where they climb out and return on a slide near by. They also have regular trails where they go around a waterfall or leave the water to travel the shore. In snow or mud they drag their tails.

The droppings are easy to identify, as they contain parts of fish and crayfish. You may find an otter toilet where large quantities of crustaceans and fish scales remain, indicating continual use for months and years. Their toilets will have a well-worn trail from the water.

In some areas otter will wad or twist grass into a little mound and use it for a scent post. These are most common near their den, or a raised area in a marsh.

Small islands and long low arms of land which extend out into rivers or lakes may have otter feeding spots, trails, or play areas.

TRAPS FOR OTTER

Otter have been taken in No. 1 traps that drowned them. This is an accident, for they can pull out of traps as large as No. 3 and No. 4 if not caught properly. The No. 4 double-spring trap and No. 4 underspring jump trap are recommended for otter trapping. The 330 Conibear also is being used in many areas. The 4½, 14, 48, and 114 Newhouse traps take otter when set for beaver. These are heavy, expensive, and very strong traps. Toothed traps are now illegal in many states, so hang them up and use them only as a talking topic.

Traps should be checked for spring strength. The traps need to be dyed to give them a dark color. A few trappers wax the traps, but this really isn't necessary.

SETS FOR OTTER

All materials should be available for drowning sets unless the Conibear is used. The drowning-set procedure is covered in Chapter 15.

Trail Set

The trail set is put where otter leave the water to go to the toilet, play area, travel trail, feeding location, or just a loafing and resting place. Set your trap where the otter leaves the water and is starting to walk. Have the trap in shallow water, preferably slightly dug in so it won't be pushed or moved. It can also be lightly covered to fool the trap thief. As long as the trap is dark, the otter won't notice it. Use an 8-to-12-pound rock fastened to the trap chain and an extra 4 to 6 feet of extension chain fastened to a good solid stake. If the drown wire is used it should be well staked in the shallow water. At the other end and 6 to 12 feet out in deep water you need a 20-to-30-pound weight fastened to the wire.

It's not wise to set traps where otter slide back into the water. The otter will be coming down the slide with its front legs folded back along its body and hind feet nearly straight back of it. Some are caught by a fold of skin, but more will pull out or snap the trap and have the devil scared out of them.

It may be necessary to make a dry-land set on a trail. Use a step-over stick to make it put a foot where you want it. The No. 4 trap should be used; if No. 3 traps are used, set two, and stake them. This way the otter is often caught by two feet. Do not use weak-springed traps.

Trail Conibear Set

Some trails are good locations for the 330 Conibear. Where otter enter the water, control wings made by pushing stakes into the dirt can be used. Have the stakes forming wings and sticking above water. A small floating pole or log will force the otter to go underwater. These wing sets should be prepared a few weeks before traps are set to let animals get used to them. An opening large enough for the otter to easily swim through should be prepared. The Conibear should have the triggers bent to right and left at about half their length. Stake the trap-spring rings solidly, having the trigger at the bottom. Have two stakes, one through each spring and between the corner edges of the lower jaws. This will make a strong, stable set. The spring-ring stakes can be wired to the floating pole for extra security. This will be similar to the controlled-channel set for beaver.

Bait and Lure Sets

Otter have been taken on bait and lures, but not in great numbers. More otter will be taken by finding their travel routes, trails, and runways.

If bait sets are made, use canned fish, fresh fish oil, or fresh fish or meat. Bait should be used near a bank or where otter will be traveling. Have the trap 6 to 8 inches back from the bait.

The traps should be set in the water. In making all otter sets in water use hip boots or work from a boat. Make the set so the otter cannot leave the water but will be forced to deeper water.

Baited Conibear traps can be used under ice. The set will work better if it is close to open water near the route otter are likely to take. Fasten a 6-inch fish on the trigger wires. The traps can be fastened to a pole flat on the bottom or to a vertical pole that extends above the ice. The poles should be secure. Have a wire or chain from the pole, if laying the trap on the bottom, or to an anchor if above the ice. Wire an anchor pole to the top of the vertical pole set.

Beaver-Dam Set

Many otter are taken while trapping beaver. The slideway over the dam and any open water at the dam edge are natural passageways for otter. The beaver sets, all being made as drowning sets, are very effective on the otter.

The one set that uses a controlled water passageway in a channel, described in Chapter 15, is an excellent otter set. The trigger wires on the 330 Conibear should be bent to the outside halfway down.

RUNNING THE LINE

Otter are seldom trapped as the main target animal. They are taken by the mink, muskrat, beaver, nutria, and raccoon trappers. When otter are taken on the line, reset the trap as it was before and treat the catch as you would a beaver.

Very few otter are taken alive, but if they are, be careful, for they don't hesitate to bite. Strike above the eyes with a killing stick, or shoot them with a .22 Short at the base of the ear or the center of the forehead.

PELT CARE

The otter is a difficult furbearer to skin, and guard hairs singe easily when exposed to sunlight. The otter is cased. Starting at the center of the hind foot, split to the anal opening from both legs. Cut around the scent gland and anal opening. Split the tail the full length on the underside and skin it out. Rough-skin the animal, for most have a good layer of fat on the hide. Cut the front feet free at the wrist. Cut the ear cartilage at the skull base. After cutting the eye and lip membrane, sever the nose cartilage and then the hide will come free.

Place the hide on the scraping board and thoroughly remove all fat and flesh. The otter skin is a tough one to flesh properly. Do not use too sharp a fleshing tool, and make sure root hairs are not exposed through the leather. When finished with the fleshing wipe the hide with a cotton cloth or paper toweling to remove grease. Repeat the wiping again after the hide is dry, for the otter hide will fat-burn easily.

A round pole or the fleshing beam used with a dull drawknife works fastest. Some trappers use a beef or horse rib bone for fleshing.

Pull the pelt over a drying board, pull it tight, and nail it well. The tail must be stretched, spread, and also nailed. The average-sized otter stretcher should be 5 feet long, 7½ inches wide at the base, and 6 inches, 13½ inches wide from the nose. The nose area should be slightly rounded and then tapered for about 6 inches. The board material should be ½ inch thick and all edges rounded and smooth.

For small otter, the board should be ½ inch narrower, and for large hides ½ inch wider. Store dried pelts in a cool place and out of the sun and bright light.

22
Care of
Pelts

The trapping of the animals and the skinning is about half of the job of the trapper. If he is to get top dollar for his catch he must be able to clean and repair the pelts, and stretch them correctly.

WASHING

There will be times when the trapper ends up with a dirty pelt. Perhaps the set was at a muddy location and the fur is coated with mud. Perhaps the animal was shot and there is blood on the fur. In either case it is a simple matter to wash the pelt to remove the unwanted material. It takes time, and the trapper should not wash unless it is necessary. But a hide that is properly washed and dried will bring just about the same money as a naturally clean hide.

Skin the animal and take the pelt directly to a pail of water. Soak well in cold or lukewarm water. Most of the mud or blood will come out readily. When all of the easy stain is out, add clear water with a small amount of a liquid detergent. Work the suds into the fur much the same as you would wash your own hair. When the fur is well lathered, rinse in clean water. Keep rinsing until the rinse water remains clear. Take the hide and work the hands down the fur from the nose to the tail, stripping out all excess water. Hang the pelt by the nose in a shady location that is exposed to the wind. When the fur is dry the pelt can be treated as any other pelt.

Skunk Scent

Some animals have a problem that is not connected with dirt. The skunk is an obvious example. The skunk will almost always throw scent when it is caught and killed, and the scent will settle on the fur. Unless the scent is removed, many fur buyers will find they have urgent business at the back of the shop when you come to sell

The authors with a few of the gray fox taken during the 1977-78 season. *(Photo: Gerry Blair)*

your catch. To clean a skunk hide, dip the hide into a can of gasoline before skinning. When the gas has dried out of the fur, skin the skunk. Now take it to the pail of water and wash it as directed for the dirty hide. The soap will remove the last traces of the gasoline and leave a pelt that looks good and smells good.

Pine Pitch

If the trapline is in pine country, the trapper will find some animals with gobs of pine sap or pitch balled in the fur. This material can usually be removed by thinning it with turpentine. Saturate a paper towel with the turpentine and let it sit on the pitch until it can be removed from the hair. Do not attempt to pull the gob of pitch away from the hair without first loosening it. Hair will come with the pitch and leave a gap in the fur. This will decrease the value of the fur as much as if the pitch had been left in, and perhaps more.

FLESHING

Most fur needs some fleshing. Some animals, such as the bobcat, put on very little fat as a rule and will need a minimum of fleshing. Others, such as the skunk, badger, and raccoon, will be very fatty and will need a lot of fleshing. Although the term "fleshing"

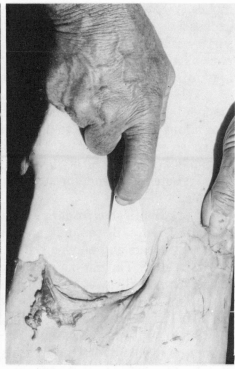

Left: The fleshing board should be about the size of the cased skin. Work from the head down. *(Photo: Gerry Blair)*
Right: A dull putty knife is used here as a flesher. Any burrs or mats in the fur will cause a tear during fleshing. *(Photos: Gerry Blair)*

brings to mind flesh, the main object of the fleshing operation is to remove the layer of fat that lies between the hide and the flesh. There is always some flesh, of course. These are small chunks and layers that are missed in the skinning. The fleshing takes them away as well as the fat. The fat and flesh must be removed if the hide is to dry properly. Fat oɪ flesh left on the hide will cause the hide to burn, and hair slip will be the result.

These are some ways of holding the fur to make the fleshing operation easier. Get a piece of 2 x 4 about 5 feet long. Round off the end and sand until all rough areas are smoothed. Also sand and smooth the edges. Nail the 2 x 4 to a support that will hold it steady. Slip the pelt, hair side in, over the board. The nose may be tacked in position if desired. The pelt will offer a work surface of 4 inches. When this is fleshed, the trapper can rotate the hide to expose a new work surface. A larger board will offer a wider work surface and will often make the job quicker. All burrs and pitch pockets must be removed before the fleshing. Otherwise the fleshing knife will catch on them and make an ugly hole.

A fleshing knife can be any dull scraper. Good fleshing knives are available from supply houses, but each trapper has his own idea about the best knife to use. A putty knife might do the job if the sharp edge is dulled and the corners rounded. Some trappers use a piece of scrap iron about a foot long with handles fitted to the ends. Whatever is used, the edge that contacts the hide should not be sharp.

Work the flesher from the nose end of the hide back toward the tail. There will be some areas that the knife will not reach. Around the ears and between the ears and the tip of the nose are two such areas. The trapper must take a sharp pocket knife to these locations and skin away the flesh and the fat. Pay careful attention to the ears. There will be hunks of flesh and glands clinging to the inside of the ears. Remove all of this, as leaving it will surely cause the skin to taint and slip. Use the knife on any part of the hide that cannot be reached with the fleshing knife.

It is possible to overflesh. Do not go down so deep with the flesher that the hair roots are disturbed.

SALT
Salt is often used as a substitute for proper fleshing. Some trappers will leave enough meat on the hide to feed the local football team and then pour a dime's worth of salt on the hide to prevent spoilage. This does not work. Most fur buyers do not want furs that have been salted. The salt slows the drying action of the hide and makes it more difficult to tan. Every pass with the salt shaker will cost the trapper some money. If salt is used at all, it should be used sparingly around the ears, and maybe on the inside of the tail. Even here, it is better to split the tail and let it air dry.

REPAIRING DAMAGED PELTS
When the hide has been washed and fleshed, it is almost ready for stretching. If there are any cuts, tears, or bullet holes in the hide the trapper should repair these first. Use heavy white thread and a large needle. Start at one end of the opening and run the needle

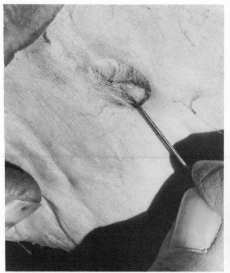 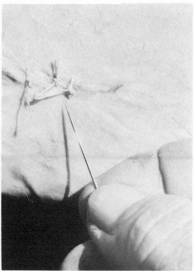

Left: Tears from bullet holes or skinning cuts should be mended. Use a waxed thread to make the job easier.
Right: When the hole is sewed, and the hide dries, the small defect will be invisible. *(Photos: Gerry Blair)*

and thread through both edges. Cut the thread, leaving enough on each end to tie a square knot. Move down about ¼ inch and repeat. Keep going until all of the opening has been sutured. When the pelt dries, the repairs will not be visible and will not detract from the value of the pelt.

Another suturing method to repair cuts caused when skinning or fleshing, or rips from road kills or bullet damage, is to use the heavy white thread and large needle and start at the inner part of a rip or one end of a cut. Have your thread waxed. Knot the loose end. Every ⅛ to ¼ inch run the needle through the flesh side, bring it up, and run it down through the flesh side nearly opposite the other suture. By doing this no fur is pulled through by the thread. Continue to the end of the cut or rip and then tie off the string end. This will also make a neat repair job and may be a timesaver.

FORCED-AIR DRYING
During rainy or damp weather, a good fan can be used to speed up drying fur of a washed pelt. After the hides are stretched fur side

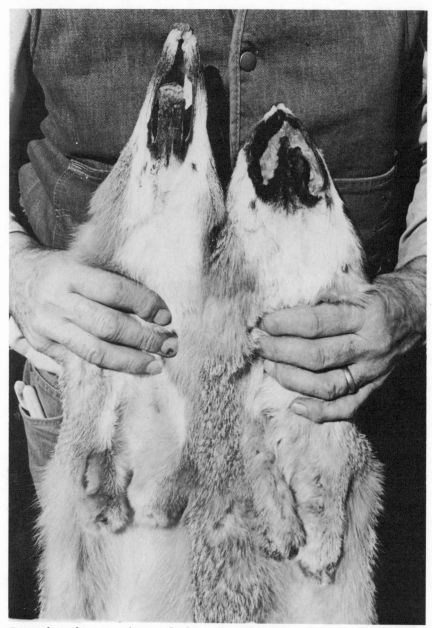

Correctly and incorrectly stretched gray fox. The pelt on the left will bring more money even though both were about the same size before stretching. (Photo: Gerry Blair)

in, drying time can be greatly reduced by the use of a fan. This method should be continued after the pelt is turned with the fur out. The fan will not only assist in drying but will also help fluff the fur to make better-looking pelts.

The fan needed will vary in size according to the number of pelts and the amount of damp weather you have to contend with. We prefer an 18-inch air circulator with a three-speed switch.

STRETCHING

The purpose of the stretching board is to allow the green pelt to dry into a shape that will take advantage of the animal's size. Some animals have very loose skin that will stretch out almost twice the size of the original animal. If a pelt was allowed to dry without being on a stretching board it would shrink and shrivel to a small and unattractive size.

Small furbearers can be stretched on the wire stretchers sold by the trapping-supply houses. Many trappers, however, are convinced that the wood stretcher permits a more exact fit of skin to stretcher, and that this extra care will return extra dollars when the fur is sold. Stretcher construction techniques are discussed in Chapter 5.

To stretch a pelt, put it on the stretcher with the fur side in. Position the nose so that it fits square on the end of the stretcher. If a wood stretcher is used, nail or tack the nose into position. Wriggle the hide until it fits evenly on the stretcher. The ears should be centered at the top and the tail should hit the center at the rear. Pull the hide as far back on the stretcher as it will go and use small nails to tack it into position. At this point only the nose and the ends of the rear legs are nailed. If the stretcher is an adjustable stretcher, spread the legs at the back until the desired shape is obtained. Tack or nail the crosspiece into position. Finish by nailing the rear legs and the nose and mouth to the board. Put the stretcher in an area out of the sun which has good air circulation. A good spot is out of doors, in the shade, where the wind can reach it. Watch that there are no flies to crawl inside the cavities and deposit eggs.

Leave the fur in this position until almost dry. Check the area around the ears and the front legs daily. These will be the last areas to dry. When the hide is almost dry, remove it from the stretcher and turn it. It should be noted that some varieties of fur

The bobcat pelt on the right was improperly stretched and will bring a lower price. *(Photo: Gerry Blair)*

are sold with the fur in. It is not necessary to turn these. When the fur is off the stretching board, push the end of the nose down inside the fur. Keep working the head down in the fur, and when the head has been reversed, reach inside the pelt from the rear end and grab the nose to pull it on through. If the fur is too dry to turn, use a wet rag or a bunch of wet paper towels to moisten the edges of the hide. This will make the hide soft enough to turn. The front legs are turned before the rest of the pelt. Use a pair of longnose pliers to reach inside the legs. Grab the end of the leg with the pliers and pull on through. When the hide has been turned it is replaced on the stretching board with the fur side out. It is nailed into place the same as it was before. The pelt is left on the board until it is completely dry. Then take it from the board and hang it in a cool airy place by the nose.

BRUSHING PELTS

When the pelts have been removed from the boards for the last time, many trappers use a wire brush to fluff the fur. Use any stiff brush to comb the hair and remove any small tangles. A small hand hair blower can be used to give the fur a last-minute fluff.

FOLDING

Dried pelts should never be folded unless it is necessary to do so to send them to market. Even then it is better to leave the hides full-stretched. If it is necessary to fold the hides, fold large hides such as coyote, bobcat, or fox one time. The fold should be in the middle of the skin.

SHIPPING

Most major fur buyers who buy by mail provide shipping tags and instructions to potential customers. The seller is more or less at the buyer's mercy in this instance, as he is not there to speak up for his fur or to contest the grading. Some fur companies will offer to keep the trapper's shipment separate until he has had a chance to accept or reject the price. If a trapper is dealing with a buy-by-mail company for the first time, he should probably take advantage of this feature. He might want his furs returned rather than accept a low price.

Only completely dry furs should be shipped. Any green fur in the packet will likely spoil from being packed, and as it spoils it

The bobcat is currently the only spotted fur available to the industry. Washing will lighten the fur and give a better contrast. *(Photo: Gerry Blair)*

will probably taint the entire shipment with the smell of rotten meat. If it is absolutely necessary to ship green hides, disregard the advice against salting. Use a light coating of salt on the inside of the hide to keep it from spoiling in transit.

Place a tag inside every bundle of furs shipped. If the outside address tag is lost, the inner tag will identify the furs. Tie a shipping tag to the outside of the container with the address and name of the fur company and with your own return address. The furs may be packaged in a cardboard box or they may be sewn into a burlap bag. The bag sometimes works best because it allows some air circulation in shipment. Furs should not be shipped in plastic bags, for any part of a pelt not totally dry will spoil and contaminate an entire shipment. The fastest method of shipment is by bus, and next-fastest by United Parcel. The slowest is parcel post. All shipments should be insured.

FREEZING
Some trappers never flesh or stretch a pelt. They skin the animal and place the green pelt in the deep freeze to await the arrival of

the fur buyer. This saves the trapper much time and work, as the fleshing and stretching operations are time-consuming. However, the buyer usually won't pay top dollar for a pelt that he has to flesh and stretch himself. You can try it both ways, if there are buyers in your area who will buy green pelts. Sell a few of the frozen ones and sell a few of the fleshed and dried ones. You will soon learn whether you're better off one way or the other.

To freeze a skin, turn it hair side out after it is removed from the animal. If it is only to be frozen a short time, roll the hide into a ball and place it inside a plastic bag. Squeeze all available air out and seal the bag with freezer tape. Place the name of the species and the date of freezing on the outside of the bag with a marking pencil. Put the bag into the deep freeze and leave it there till the buyer arrives. When taking the hide from the freezer do not try to straighten the hide until it is completely thawed. Forcing a frozen hide open will damage it.

23
Marketing of Pelts

Payday comes for the trapper when he takes his fur to market. It can come several times during the season, or if it is his choice, one time at the end of the trapping year. The amount of the check depends largely on the number of furs taken, the value of the individual species, the primeness of the fur, and the manner in which the fur was handled. Well-handled prime fur should bring top dollar. Unfortunately, this is not always the case. Where and how the trapper sells his catch often determines whether he has a good financial year or a bad one. Some trappers may sell their fur to the wrong buyer and sacrifice most of their profit.

Some fur buyers use every bit of skill they possess to get the fur from the trapper at the cheapest possible price. They will low-grade the fur to the point that the trapper decides to give up trapping completely. Why trap, if there is no market for the product? Some buyers pay the low price because they do not know the business and must allow a wide margin of profit to survive. Others may know the business well and pay the low price because they are in a position to take advantage of the trapper. In either case the trapper ends up the loser. The fur buyer who regularly takes advantage of his customers will not stay in business for any great while. When a trapper is stung a time or two, he takes his business to a more honest merchant, one who is willing to pay a fair price for good fur.

Most fur buyers, it should be noted, are honest men. As merchants, they must buy lower than they sell. The trapper should not begrudge the buyer his honest profit. The trapper, though, also needs his profit, and the buyer should pay enough for the catch to make the trapping worthwhile.

A fur trapper has four general options in selling fur. He can

Bill Musgrove with a part of the 1977-78 catch. The fur has been bundled for transportation. *(Photo: Gerry Blair)*

sell to a local buyer; he can sell by mail to an out-of-town firm; he can put his catch up as a lot in a fur auction; or he can market his fur through a fur combine.

LOCAL BUYERS

The local man usually gives the small trapper the best price for his few furs. He is probably an acquaintance, and if the community is a small one, a friend. To stay in business he must develop a reputation for fair deals. If he does not he soon runs out of customers and closes his doors.

The local buyer usually has had experience as a trapper. He knows local trapping conditions and local furs. At times he has a stock of trapping supplies available to help out the trapper. He is available to buy a fur or a few furs if the trapper needs some quick cash to get traps or gas. Many times the local buyer makes regular visits to different points in the trapping territory to deliver supplies and buy fur.

As an experienced trapper and fur handler himself, the local buyer is often a valuable source of information to the beginning trapper. He can advise on trapping and fur-handling techniques. The new trapper has a chance to improve his skills by asking the advice of this experienced individual.

When dealing with the local buyer, the trapper is often able to sell his fur in a condition that would not be acceptable to other buyers. Some local men will buy unskinned or frozen pelts. The price received for these fresh hides or unskinned animals often approaches the price received for well-handled fur.

The beginning trapper has one further advantage in dealing with the local man. He is there when the furs are graded and has the opportunity to discuss the grading techniques with the buyer. If the buyer undergrades, the trapper has a chance to protest the grading and learn what defects appear to the buyer. If the trapper is not satisfied with the grading he can take his furs and leave.

SELLING BY MAIL

If the local man does not offer a fair price, or if the community does not have a local buyer, the trapper may want to sell his fur by mail. Selling by mail, the trapper will learn, has a number of disadvantages. The first problem is possible loss of, or damange to, the fur during shipment. Much of this problem can be eliminated by shipping by United Parcel rather than by mail. UPS offers a fairly fast transport, and if the packet is lost or damaged, has a settlement procedure that will leave the trapper happy. Mail, on the other hand, is slow, and the fur is likely to be damaged. If the fur is damaged or lost, the trapper will surely have an ulcer before he sees one penny of Uncle Sam's money. Shipping the packet of fur by bus is also possible. Bus is probably the fastest way to get the fur into the hands of the buyer, but again, there is quite a legal hassle if the furs are lost.

There are other problems in shipping fur. The trapper is not there when the fur is graded and he must take the buyer's word on the quality of the pelts. Some greedy buyers may reduce the quality of every skin a grade or two. He may label some shedders that are not. He may be able to see singeing and rubbing that no one else can notice. He may also call a large a medium, and a medium a small.

Some experienced trappers grade their own fur before shipment and set a minimum price they will accept. There have been instances where the trappers were certain that the returned furs were not the ones sent to the buyer. The buyer, they felt, had kept their prime lot of fur and had returned a batch of low-quality skins. It is possible for a buyer to do this but it is not likely. Such practices are seldom seen in today's fur dealings.

The trapper who sells by shipment should check out his intended market as thoroughly as possible. Reliable companies will advertise in *Fur Takers of America Journal*, *Voice of the Trapper* (which is published by the National Trappers Association), or magazines such as *Fur Fish and Game*.

On the day that the furs are shipped, write a letter to the company. List the date the packet was sent, the method of transportation, the type of container used, the amount and types of fur, the estimated value of the packet, and your trapping license number. If the packet does not reach the buyer when it should, he is in a position to advise you of that fact so that you can lose no time tracing the shipment.

Reliable fur companies will hold a fur shipment for ten days. Many buyers also call the trapper by telephone to quote the price they offer for the packet. If the price is not acceptable the return postage is generally prepaid.

When looking over a fur price list, most young trappers set their sights for the top-of-the-line prices. Most packets of pelts, if properly handled, will earn only a medium or high-medium quotation. If there are defects such as unprimeness, damage, singeing, or rubbing, the price will go much lower.

Many large buyers will automatically send a check on the same day that the furs are received and graded. If the trapper cashes the check he has made the deal. If the company advertises a ten-day hold, however, the trapper has a chance to return the check and ask for the return of his fur.

FUR AUCTIONS

Many trappers are becoming aware of the advantages of the fur auction. With a number of buyers competing for the same lot of fur the seller is more likely to get the top dollar for his pelts. At small local auctions, with only one or two serious buyers, this advantage is often not realized.

One of the largest of the current fur auctions is the Dominion Soudack Fur Auction held in Winnipeg, Manitoba. During the February 1978 sale, 125 foreign and domestic buyers competed for the fur. Many auctions are held in the continental United

States during the trapping season. They may be operated by a group of trappers or by a buyers' organization. The auctions are usually advertised in the trapping magazines, journals, and newspapers. Listed will be time, location, and the prices paid for each species at the previous month's auction.

To sell at an auction, the trapper must report with his furs a day or two before the auction. His lot of furs will be released to the auction manager. In many cases the furs are shipped to the auction and the seller does not have to attend. A minimum acceptable price will be listed on the auction form for each of the packets offered. Many times the seller puts *SELL* on the form and his furs automatically go to the highest bidder. If a minimum price is listed, and no buyer reaches that price, the packet of fur is not sold and is shipped back to the trapper. Most of the auctions will hold the furs until the next auction if the trapper indicates he wants that done. The auction house takes a percentage of the total price of the fur sold as its commission.

Each lot of fur is usually comprised of the species of fur sent to the auction. If the trapper sent eighty coyote, thirty-two bobcat, and one striped skunk to the auction, his fur would be divided into three lots—one for each species.

The advantage of the fur auction is most apparent when the trapper has a large quantity of fur to sell. Even then there must be enough buyers at the sale to induce spirited bidding. The trapper will then receive top dollar.

The disadvantage of auction selling, of course, is the commission kept by the auctioneer for the handling and selling. If the auction has only a few bidders, competition may not surface and the trapper gets a low price for his fur. In some instances, if there are only one or two bidders with money, they may conspire to low-bid the fur to get the lot at the cheapest price. If this happens, and the trapper has to pay the auction commission, he may get less for his fur than if he had sold locally.

FUR COMBINES

The fur combine is becoming popular with many trappers. More furs are sold by the state units of the Fur Takers of America, for example, than by any other organization.

The largest fur-combine seller is the Oregon Territorial Council. It is managed and operated by the Fur Takers of America,

Buyers inspecting fur lots at a fur combine sale. *(Photo: Bill Musgrove)*

Oregon Chapter. The organization is trapper-owned and trapper-operated. A single three- or four-day sale has seen more than a quarter of a million dollars in fur change hands.

These sales are operated as auctions. The lots are handled by sealed bid. A display fee and a percentage of the selling price is paid to the council.

Here again, if there are not enough buyers with money, the trapper can be hurt. Too few buyers means no competition, and low prices will result. Check the prices paid at previous auctions to learn how well the sale draws buyers.

DECIDING HOW TO SELL

The best advice, then, is to sell locally if there is a local buyer who will give good prices and if you have only a small amount of fur to be sold. The local buyer, more than likely, takes the fur bought from trappers to one of the auctions or combines, or is buying for a larger fur company. He must buy the fur cheap enough to allow a profit at the auction. If you have made a large catch you might do better to cut out the middleman and take your fur directly to the auction. By attending personally you should realize an extra profit. Too, you will be there to give your fur a last-minute grooming that will allow it to look its best. And the fur auctions are fun. You have a chance to mingle with other trappers. New friendships can be formed and old friendships renewed. The exchange of information allows all trappers a new insight into the business. By comparing your pelts with other lots you can gain an insight into your own fur-handling skills. The trip will make you a better taker and handler of fur. And it will probably put more money in your pocket.

WHEN TO SELL

When the fur is sold might make a big difference in the number on the paycheck. There is no hard and fast rule because there are too many variables. The early fur sales usually do not see much in the way of new fur. Most of the fur sold is left over from the last season. Buyers, as a rule, do not dip deep into their wallets for holdover fur.

By midseason the year's prices have began to stabilize. There is fresh fur hitting the market and domestic buyers are beginning to build an inventory of the fur they have contracted to foreign buyers. The prices continue to harden, and good prices for most species will be paid by January and February. This coincides with the prime time for many furs and may have something to do with the solid market. Some years, the prices peak at the last sale of the season. Buyers who held off buying now have to bid high to fulfill their contract commitments. Other years the prices peak early and go soft at season's end. The market may be flooded with a particular species and the price will plummet. If this happens, in all probability there will be a lot of holdover fur to be sold early next season. The prices, if this happens, may stay low through most of the following season for that species. Watch the prices paid at auctions quoted in the magazines. The trapper soon learns the current season's trend of fur prices. He should sell when the price seems fair to him.

If the small trapper does not have room at his home to store a large catch of fur he will be forced into selling the fur in small lots. This sometimes works out to his advantage, as he receives the entire spectrum of prices from high to low and ends the season with a healthy average.

FUR GRADING

The buyer considers a number of features when he grades fur. Size is one grading factor. A big prime fur brings more money than a small prime fur if both are well handled. The trapper gets the best dollar for his fur by stretching it properly. The hide should not shrink more than necessary during the drying process. The hide should not be overstretched, however. Overstretching thins the hide and the fur, and the trapper loses more than he gains. To grade for size the buyer measures the pelt for length from tip of nose to hips, measures the width of the hide at the shoulders, and measures the width at the hips. These measurements place the pelt into a small, medium, or large category, or a subdivision of those categories.

Color

Most furbearers have some color variation within the same range and might have a radical color variation as the ranges change. The bobcat, for instance, is dark-colored in part of its Pacific Coast range. The cat of southwest and north-central Canada and the United States, however, is much lighter in color and has an almost white underbelly.

Fashion demands control fur prices, and at the present time light-colored fur is fashionable. The lighter cats are more in demand and bring a substantially higher price. The same can be said of the coyote, which has a color range over most of its range that grades from a light silver to an auburn. The lighter skins bring the best price. Fashion, of course, is a fickle standard. Color preferences can change from season to season.

Quality

To determine quality the buyer checks the length of the underfur, the length of the guard hair, and the overall gloss of the pelt. Fur taken from certain geographic areas often rates consistently high in quality. Fur from the same species taken 100 miles away might score consistently low. Diet, habitat, cover, and temperature are among the determining factors in producing quality fur.

The quality grading is mostly an eyeball judgment. The buyer considers the overall appearance of the pelt to rate the eye appeal. The trapper will get the best money for his fur when it has been properly handled. Wash any fur if color or texture can be improved. Many times, as with a bobcat skin, washing lightens the fur and the trapper receives a better price on color. The washing

Bobcat hides tied for transportation to the auction. Note the clean contrasty appearance of the belly fur. (*Photo: Gerry Blair*)

also brightens the fur and brings a few extra dollars on quality. The wash may also take out "deducts" such as bloodstains, mud-balls, and, with a little turpentine, pitch balls.

The skunk pelt that smells like a skunk is hard to sell. If the stinky hide is shipped with other fur the whole batch ends up with a skunky odor. Make it a practice to descent all skunk hides with gasoline, as described earlier in this chapter. The skunk pelt, and any pelts that ride to market with the skunk, scores better on quality if the grader doesn't have to hold his nose while he grades.

The trapper can give his pelts a last-minute grooming that improves the quality grade. Furs when stored or shipped develop a crushed look. Cowlicks will develop. Use a stiff bristle brush or wire brush to fluff the hair. It looks thicker and thereby brings a better price.

DAMAGE
Most fur damage can be repaired, as explained in Chapter 22. Bullet holes, tears, and skinning cuts can be sewed before the hide is stretched. Pine-pitch snarls can be removed with turpentine. Bloodstains can be rinsed out with cold water. Tangles and burrs can be removed with a little effort. Other defects cannot be repaired but can be prevented by careful fur handling. Meat chunks left after skinning often taint the hide and cause hair slippage. Too much fat on the hide will do the same. Even a hide that is properly skinned and fleshed may have hair slippage if it is in too warm a room, particularly if the room has poor air circulation. Salt on the hide will keep it from spoiling but may cause other problems. If the buyer lives in a damp climate the salt in the hide will attract moisture from the air and the hide will go limp. A hide that is removed too soon from the stretcher shrinks and wrinkles. If the drying board is not the correct dimensions the hide dries to an irregular shape and points are deducted. When a hide is over-stretched the hide and the fur will be thin and quality points will be lost.

PRIME FUR
Prime fur is fur that is taken in the winter months when cold weather causes the fur to thicken, and the hide is thinner and light-colored. Primeness refers to the condition of the hide and not the fur. When a hide is prime the inside of the hide will be a

The fur on this howling coyote is degrading. The lower hips show rubbing and the fur on the top of the back shows curl and shedding. *(Photo: U.S. Fish and Wildlife Service)*

creamy color. This color stays even after the hide is fleshed and dried. A hide that is prime is thin. A hide that is not prime is thick, with thin fur and heavy guard hair, and the hide has a gray color. The color comes from the ends of the hair follicles showing through the bottom of the hide. The hide also dries a gray color.

At certain times of the year the hide may be prime but the fur is degrading. Some animals rub the hip area in the spring to rid themselves of the thick winter coat. This rubbing is most notice-able in coyote and fox. As the summer sun becomes warmer, the guard hair on many furbearers begins to curl from the heat of the sun. This is a condition called singeing and it will degrade the fur. It is better to pull the traps when either of these conditions is noticed in trapped animals. Leave them for next winter when the fur will be prime and full and will bring you a worthwhile return for your efforts.

24
Recordkeeping

Most trappers trap because they want to be in the field among the animals. Many avoid the keeping of records because it takes them inside and puts them behind a desk. But a certain amount of recordkeeping is necessary to run a fur-trapping business.

TAX RECORDS

Any money that the trapper realizes from the trapline is subject to federal income tax. The state will probably want a few furs also, if your state is one of the many with a state income tax. To keep from paying more than his fair share, the trapper is allowed to claim certain deductions—expenses he has incurred in the business of trapping. To be able to support those expenses the trapper must keep certain records. Many times the fur buyer is required by law to report the sums paid to individual trappers. This gives the tax men the amount of money made from the trapline. Unless proper records are available to support expenses, the trapper will be expected to pay tax on the total paycheck.

Vehicle

The vehicle, or vehicles, that a trapper uses on the line can be a major part of his tax deduction. The vehicle may be a four-wheel-drive truck, a snowmobile, or a motorcycle. If the trapper uses a horse, he is allowed to deduct certain parts of the upkeep from his tax bill.

Most of the time the vehicle used on the trapline is used partially for the business and partially for pleasure. The law allows a deduction for that part used on the trapline. If a vehicle is used solely for trapping, then the entire cost of the vehicle plus the maintenance costs are deductible.

The gasoline and oil used to run the business are also a legitimate expense. The trapper may want to keep track of the amount of miles devoted to the line and take a mileage allowance. Others prefer to keep records of the exact amount of money spent for gas, oil, tires, and maintenance and to claim the dollar amount. An easy way of recordkeeping is to obtain a gasoline-company credit card in the name of the trapping enterprise. Charge all line expenses to the card. The credit-card company will do the recordkeeping. Its itemized statements will provide the documentation to support vehicle expenses.

The original cost of the vehicle can also be claimed as a tax expense. If the vehicle is used solely for the trapline, the trapper may take the entire purchase price as a deduction. Usually, on an item such as a vehicle, the purchase price is prorated over a number of years. He is allowed to claim depreciation for the equipment each year. If the vehicle is used only partly for the trapline, the trapper can deduct a part of the cost. If the trapping season lasts six months of the year, and the trapper uses the vehicle exclusively for trapping during that time, he could claim that the vehicle was used 50 percent of the time for trapping. This would allow the trapper to use the vehicle the other half of the year for pleasure purposes. If the vehicle was put away at the end of the season and not used for pleasure the trapper would be able to claim the entire cost as a deduction.

Do not disregard the less obvious vehicle costs. Many trappers will claim the obvious costs such as purchase price, gas and oil, tires, and maintenance, but will forget the vehicle license fees and insurance.

Equipment

The equipment that the trapper buys to do the job of trapping is also deductible. Again, proper receipts must be maintained or the deductions may be disallowed. Keep the sales receipt, and if it does not list the nature of the purchase, write a brief description of the item on the back of the sales slip. Traps are an obvious deduction. Packsacks, scrapers, stretchers, knives, showshoes, scents and lures, firearms, and all other purchases made for the line are deductible expenses. Any special clothing that is bought for use on the line, and that is not an ordinary item of dress, may also be a correct deduction. The price of this book, as a matter of fact, could be a legitimate business expense, like any money paid for other publications, books, or magazines, that were bought to increase your knowledge of the business.

Freight and Postage

Any expenses for postage, either letters or packages, and sending your furs to market are deductible. If the furs are taken to market personally, the cost of the trip itself is deductible.

Fees and Licenses

The money spent to buy a trapping license, and, if one is required, a business license, is also deductible. So are any membership fees paid to professional groups such as state and national trapping associations. If the trapper attends an annual convention of the association he will be able to claim a part or all of his trip expenses as a business expense.

Lost Traps

Do not fail to record the number of traps lost or stolen on the line during the season. The trapper might deduct the entire cost of the trap as a casualty loss. He might do better to buy a new trap and deduct the new cost. Traps, like everything else, have increased in value over the years. You may not be able to buy a new one for the same price you paid for the old one. Include losses of other equipment such as stakes, drags, and grapples.

Sales

The trapper should also record the money collected from the sale of furs, and the sale of any subsidiary parts of the furbearer such as urine, castors, scents, or claws. Keep a record of money collected, date of sale, purchaser, and type of furbearer or product. If you hire an accountant to keep your records and prepare your tax statement, the cost of the accountant is also a legitimate business expense.

REPORTS

Many state fish and game departments require annual reports by all licensed trappers. The reports are used by the department to determine the number of furbearers being taken, and will to a large degree be used to set future seasons and bag limits. No trapper wants to trap a species to extinction, or to trap it to such a low level that its future existence is threatened. The trapper should, therefore, fully cooperate with the game departments in their efforts to manage the wildlife resources. If nothing else, it is good business. Proper management will ensure a good supply of game for times to come. The trapper cannot trap if there is nothing there to trap. He has an important stake in the wise management of furbearers.

Generally, the trapper reports ask for the numbers trapped of each species, the location where trapped, sex, age, condition, and sometimes method used.

The records that the trapper keeps will help him when it comes time to fill out his income tax. They will also be helpful in fulfilling the legal requirements of state reports. The good trapper will use the records in one other way. By reviewing his records on a yearly basis he will be able to pinpoint areas and sets that were the best producers last season. If he is a good businessman he will concentrate on those areas when he goes back to the line. High catches usually indicate good habitat and fur population.

Index